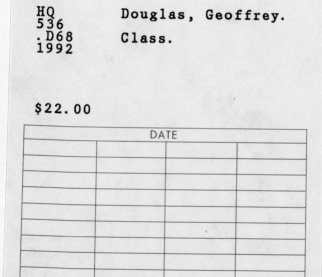

HQ
536
.D68
1992

Douglas, Geoffrey.

Class.

$22.00

CLASS

Geoffrey Douglas

Henry Holt and Company
New York

CLASS

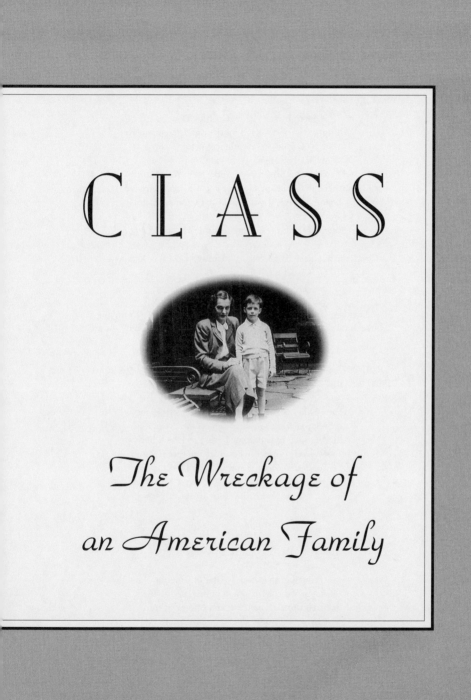

*The Wreckage of
an American Family*

Published by Henry Holt and Company, Inc.,
115 West 18th Street, New York, New York 10011.
Published in Canada by Fitzhenry & Whiteside Limited,
91 Granton Drive, Richmond Hill, Ontario L4B 2N5.

Library of Congress Cataloging-in-Publication Data
Douglas, Geoffrey.
Class : the wreckage of an American family / Geoffrey Douglas.—
1st ed.
p.   cm.
Includes bibliographical references.
1. Family—United States—Case studies.   2. Problem families—
United States—Case studies.   3. Upper classes—United States—Case
studies.   4. Douglas, Geoffrey.   I. Title.
HQ536.D68   1992
306.85′0973—dc20   92-12561
ISBN 0-8050-1737-2   CIP

Henry Holt books are available at special discounts
for bulk purchases for sales promotions, premiums,
fund-raising, or educational use. Special editions
or book excerpts can also be created to specification.
For details contact: Special Sales Director,
Henry Holt and Company, Inc., 115 West 18th Street,
New York, New York 10011.

First Edition—1992

Designed by Katy Riegel

Printed in the United States of America
Recognizing the importance of preserving the
written word, Henry Holt and Company, Inc.,
by policy, prints all of its first editions
on acid-free paper. ∞

1   3   5   7   9   10   8   6   4   2

To Archie and Ellie—

with love and sorrow

Author's Note

This is a story of a marriage—my parents'—and of the time and class that framed it. Both memoir and social history, it is a mixture, sometimes blurred, of memory and fact.

Memory is selective, the more so when decades have passed. Still, for most things in the lives of most of us, it is the only record that survives.

I have been blessed in the telling of this story to have had my own remembrances augmented (sometimes set straight) by those of others, as well as by a wealth of letters, photos, diaries, records, and keepsakes. From these many rich sources, I have done my best to resurrect the spirit and fabric of a marriage that ended nearly forty years ago.

It was a marriage endowed—then corrupted—by rank and privilege, in a time when America still mythologized its rich. The false promises and empty messages on which it rested—the sanctity of a "good name," the license of its bearer to redefine moral law—destroyed more lives than my parents', though perhaps none more nakedly or with a wreckage more widely strewn.

For me, these messages exploded early. Class didn't carry much weight in the 1960s, which made "establishment" a vulgarism and put suffixes at the end of "elite." I learned, by my college years, to mute my origins.

But among the "good names" in the forties and fifties—my parents' era, the last good years for old money in America—the New York Social Register was a holy glue. They filled our living room through the weekends of my childhood, these generals who'd won their stars without training or trial. The world they shared with my parents was lonely and misshapen, its perils were too often mistaken for codes.

I have recast that world as nearly as its distance has allowed. I do not pretend to absolute truth, nor, certainly, to completeness. My story leaves gaps that no memory or record can fill, and questions that no one but ghosts could answer today.

I have tried to be true to these ghosts. That standard, above all others, has guided every word.

The names of certain persons, no longer living, have been changed, as have those of family members who survive them. With one exception, the men and women whose voices, views, and remembrances appear on these pages are named correctly when they are named at all. To each of them I am deeply grateful:

George Constable, Bill Reed, Ruth Savage, Jack Reed, Ginny Rotan, and Audrey Lake for their memories of my mother's early years; Robert Grosjean, for allowing me the use of his letters to her, and his remembrances of their days together, and of my father.

Peggy Douglas, who gave generously of her time, her memories, and her husband's library; Ernest McAneny, for his recollections of my uncle, his unstinting assistance in gathering my father's school records, and his fond depictions of Riverdale in the early years; my half brother, Jimmy Douglas, for his early memories of the father we share.

And the witnesses to the later years: Cynthia Bangs Crocker, a recurring voice in these pages, who shared her sense of both my parents—apart and together—as well as her insights on their marriage and the values and perils of the times they lived in; Ruth and Harlow Savage, who responded to my inquiries with a generosity I had long ago come to count on; my sister, Lea (Eleanor) Douglas, who added her voice to my own in recalling the feelings and events we dug together to unearth.

The written sources that aided my search were many and diverse. Some public, some private, some even handwritten.

Besides my mother's photo albums, her suitcase of letters and mementos, and my grandfather's lifetime journal—which served, collectively, as my starting point—I relied for background on the following sources, among others:

Independent: A Biography of Lewis W. Douglas, by Robert Paul Browder and Thomas G. Smith (Alfred A. Knopf, 1986); *Once in Golconda,* by John Brooks (Harper & Row, 1969); *Manhattan '45,* by Jan Morris (Oxford University Press, 1987); *Old Money,* by Nelson W. Aldrich, Jr. (Knopf, 1988); *Journals and Reminiscences of James Douglas, M.D.,* edited by his son (privately printed, New York, 1910); *Alexander Reed and His Descendants,* compiled and edited by Alexander Preston Reed (privately printed, Pittsburgh, Pennsylvania, 1960); *The Patten Genealogy,* by Malcolm Clark Patten (Powell and Taylor Publishing, 1990).

Periodical sources include: *The Yale Alumni News, The New York Times,* the New York *Daily News,* the New York *Journal and American,* as well as several publications excerpted in my grandfather's journal.

I am grateful also for the assistance provided me by the following schools and institutions, each of which has made its records available:

Douglas Hospital, Quebec, Canada; the Riverdale School, Riverdale, New York; St. Paul's School, Concord, New Hampshire; the Yale University alumni office, New Haven, Connecticut; Miss Porter's School, Farmington, Connecticut; the Buckley School, New York, New York; the Institute of Living, Hartford, Connecticut.

But among all my sources, private and public, there are perhaps none to which I owe a greater debt than to the Silver Hill Foundation in New Canaan, Connecticut, at which my mother was a patient over several stretches during the final two years of her life. Her doctors' records of their sessions with her, some sixty-odd pages on microfilm, were my richest single source for insight and background on her marriage and its destruction. Without the detail these records provide, my story would be paler by far.

And finally, to those who believed along the way:

My agent, Philip Spitzer, whose vision planted the seed; my editor, Cynthia Vartan, for her faith, her intelligence, and the precision of her pencil; my friends at the Breadloaf Writers' Conference, especially Rick Hawley, Ron Powers, and Frankie Wright, whose advice and gentle nudgings have made this a better book; Gay Eggers, an advocate and critic from the (way back) beginnings; my sister, Lea, without whose shared belief the task would have been harder.

My son, Sam Reed Douglas, who never knew his grandparents, but taught me, at nine pounds fifteen ounces, the lesson they never learned from me.

And Cathy, my ally of allies, whose love, faith, and understanding have been my ticket from one day to the next.

CLASS

A child of riches is not at the beginning of anything. He or she is all outcome, ending, goal. And not of his own efforts or her own dreams, but of someone else's . . . the accidental and largely unfortunate consequence of someone else's success in the race . . .

—<u>Old Money</u> by Nelson W. Aldrich, Jr.

People were always glad to see them, for, if they were the pathetic grasshoppers of some gorgeous economic summer, they somehow had it in their power to remind one of good things——good places, games, food and company——and the ardor with which they looked for friends on railroad platforms could perhaps be accounted for by the fact that they were only looking for a world that they understood.

—"Just One More Time" by John Cheever

A Prologue

The Institute of Living
Hartford, Conn.
May 1964

Eight or nine doctors in suits, all of them men, all but one of them strangers to me, sit around a table. None are talking when I arrive, and none—except the eminent doctor, who sits at the head—will speak a word while I am in the room. Most of them are young— except the eminent, who is perhaps fifty—though none nearly as young as I. I am nineteen.

The doctors are introduced around the table. Each one nods in turn, some smiling tightly, as his name is announced by the eminent, who then introduces himself. He is director of psychiatry at a Midwest hospital, and has written several books.

He summarizes my case: in the Institute five months, dysfunctional on arrival, college dropout, both parents dead, mother a suicide, father an alcoholic. There is more, but these are the essentials.

He begins the questioning. The younger doctors take notes; my own doctor, who sits across from me, will not meet my eyes.

I am nervous—who would not be nervous?—and answer mostly by rote: I left college because I had no interest, wrote bad checks to cover gambling debts. . . . I don't *know* what matters to me, mostly nothing, sometimes sex or poker, sometimes a book. . . . I have no wish to die. . . . I talk of suicide mostly to watch reactions. . . . I was sent here by an uncle, who said I needed help. . . . I am not sick. . . . I am sick if you say so. . . . I don't remember my mother's death, I rarely think about my mother. . . . I don't *know* if you'd call her attractive—what kind of question is that?—she was my mother. . . . I suppose she loved me, she was my mother. . . . I never think about her. . . . I think about my father sometimes, he only died last year. . . . I have answered these questions before. . . .

"Always the same way," says the eminent.

"It's the only way I know."

"The only way you *care* to know."

"What is this about?"

"Your doctor said you were bright. You *are* bright, but you are not brave. You are a coward. Do you know that you are a coward?"

"I don't know what you mean."

"You are a coward. You cower from truth. You are afraid to look at it, afraid of what you might see."

"What truth?"

"Many truths. Many, many truths. You cannot be well—you cannot be free—until you face them."

"Such as?"

"Your mother was a *whore*."

I cannot answer. I look to my doctor for help; he plays with his pencil and looks down. The other doctors are watching my face.

"Your father was worse. An adulterer, an alcoholic. A hedonist. Do you know what a hedonist is? Yes, of course you do. A hedonist has no values. He believes in nothing. He pursues only pleasure."

I am shaking now, almost crying. But I do not speak or move.

"*Listen* to me! You are being told the *truth*. Your parents cared *nothing* for you. They ignored you, your father beat you, they surrendered your care to nurses. They were weak, hopelessly weak. They cared only for themselves.

"What do you think of *that*? Does it make you angry? . . . No, I can see not."

"You are a liar." It is all I can think to say.

Salvaged Treasures

One

In a small, black suitcase, no larger across than a standard briefcase and perhaps twice as wide, my mother kept all the things she held most dear. It is a derelict today: the "Genuine Cow Hide" lining torn and peeling, the top nearly separated from its frame, the sides buckled and held together by twine. But the latches still snap smartly when you pop them, and my mother's maiden-name initials ("E.S.R.") are still plainly visible, in painted silver letters, beneath the handle.

There is no theme or chronology to what she hoarded here. Twenty-two years are spanned, more than half her lifetime, a puzzling hodgepodge of letters, photos, old school essays, documents, and keepsakes. It is impossible to guess, in sorting through it today, what standards she applied to preciousness.

There are small, leather-bound editions (copyright 1920) of the Episcopal Hymnal and Book of Common Prayer, both surprisingly well-worn (religion, as far as I knew, was never a staple of my mother's life); several studio proofs of her in evening dress or cruisewear, dating from her days as a fashion model; a three-month contract with MGM, March 1935, assuring her a hundred and fifty dollars a week and free passage to Culver City, California, in exchange for her services as "a motion picture actor in motion pictures of various types"; a half-dozen photos, several with notes attached ("Dear Ellie: Send your picture—*of course* I want it"), of jut-jawed, wonderfully groomed young men who passed briefly through her life. Bracelet charms and diving medals; six months' worth of transatlantic love letters from a smitten young Belgian who nearly won her heart; the florists' cards that accompanied my father's courtship roses. A sheaf of snapshots of my sister and me, as baby and toddler, together with some schoolboy art and block-print scrawlings; her "re-education" notebook from the mental hospital in which she spent much of the last two years of her life.

And finally, posted from New Zealand three months before her death and less than a month after my father had moved out, a letter from her oldest friend offering advice against despair: "You, darling, are coming to the end of a long and terrible fight . . . take each day as it comes. . . . I don't care how many pills you take right now, but take it easy on the liquor."

Prayers, dreams, accommodation, survival: the slippage of her life. Her passage through them, over these twenty-two years of stored memories, was no doubt seamless and gradual, as it is for us all, like the passing of seasons. In the suitcase, though, it is as stark and vivid as the photos she kept there. I wonder if sometime, perhaps toward the end, in adding a new keepsake or rereading an old letter, she might have seen this too—and if she did, what she felt, if this was part of what destroyed her.

I hardly knew my mother. It seems almost heresy to write this, but it couldn't help but have been so. I saw her nearly every day when she was home, often several times: brief, foreshortened glimpses on my way to or from the park with Nanny; in the hallway on my way to bath or dinner—always with Nanny, though there were many nannies, some called by different names: Greenie, Marie, Miss Parish—on weekend evenings as, pajama-clad, I passed hors d'oeuvres in our living room to guests who pinched my cheeks and gave me quarters, sometimes at bedtime for a story and a squeeze ("Snug as a bug in a rug").

But these were passings only. Swift, often tender, almost never fulfilling, like the passings of others whose presence filled my life—my father, our maid Bea, the cocktail guests, our doormen George and Pat—only more precious by far.

There were exceptions. Once every year, a week or so before the start of school, I would go with her to Best's on Fifth Avenue to shop for clothes (nannies, no matter how dependable, weren't to be relied on in the matter of wardrobes). Light blue, starchy button-downs, a blue blazer, trousers, socks, and shorts. And afterward to the barbershop, downstairs at the St. Regis—"Neck like a tree trunk, or your ears will get snip-snipped"—where I sat on a booster chair in a row of old men with soap-covered faces under pin-striped sheets. The room smelled of talc and hair pomade, and the cheap perfume of the blond manicure ladies with big bosoms under tight white dresses, who chewed gum and winked at me while they held the old men's hands and scraped their nails with what I thought were tongue depressors.

There was always a treat afterward. Once it was FAO Schwarz to buy me a toy, another time—or maybe the same one—the monkey house at the Central Park Zoo. She held my hand in the street, we rode in taxis with jump seats. On our last trip together, before my fourth-grade year, the week before her death, we went for milk and pie at the Schrafft's on Fifty-seventh Street and she taught me the meaning of à la mode.

Sometimes, on nights when my father was away ("in Albany, making laws," was the standard assurance) and she was going out for the evening—I never knew where or with whom—Nanny would bring me to her, and I would sit on their bed, or on the blue chaise next to her dressing table, and watch her prepare. Lipstick, mascara, beauty spot, combing, perfume.

She always seemed harried, bustled continually, and would remind me often of how late she would be. Still, we talked: of school, sports, my father's job—"He's not a lawyer, he *makes* laws, there's a difference"—the war in Korea. And she seemed at least to be taking part.

She had invented a mnemonic for use on these nights:

> *Comb, compact, cigarettes*
> *Kleenex, keys, matches, money*
> *Three C's, two K's, two M's, make ready.*

It was my job—on cue, when she opened her purse to signal the end of the readying process—to recite this. Sometimes, I suppose if time permitted, the keys or Kleenex would be missing and I would get a second chance. I don't remember if this was the case the night before the morning she died, but I know that I watched her get ready and that I said my lines at least once.

But weekend mornings were the most treasured—though again, only when my father was not home.

They worked always the same way, when they happened at all. Sometime around noon—my mother seldom rose before noon, weekend or not—the buzzer would ring in the pantry, a signal to Bea to bring coffee and the *Trib*. A minute or two after this (if we hadn't left already for the park, the zoo, or some museum), Nanny would give me the cue and I would knock—"lightly, lightly, your mother isn't deaf"—on the door of my parents' room.

I would wait for her answer, then open it, just wide enough to insert my head. My mother, from her place on the bed, would regard me quizzically for a moment, pretending confusion, then pucker her face and act delighted, as if her oldest friend had come to call.

"Join me in the comics?" she would say, or "Anyone for Dick Tracy?"—and I would walk around to her side of the bed to collect my kiss, then take my place on my father's vacant side.

For the next hour or more—or so it seems in remembering, it may have been only half that long—we would read aloud, talk and trade sections: she always in a white nightgown with a pot of coffee at her side, lighting one cigarette off another, the pages splayed across the bedding with a randomness I can still see clearly.

Dick Tracy, Mandrake the Magician, Terry and the Pirates. Afterward, she would move on to the rest of the paper while I would blow imaginary smoke rings from her cigarette holders, reapply her beauty spot with the pencil she would give me, or fold newspaper airplanes, wing them out at her from under her dressing table, then crouch like a thief behind the pleating. Sometimes, on Sundays, we bet dimes on next week's sequels.

I can't imagine, knowing what I know today, that no inkling of her torment reached my senses. I must have felt—at least—her languor, the spirit failing as the will ran down. She was heartsick, every minute. Paralyzed half the time. I was eight, then nine. How blind could I have been?

But memory is deceitful. And our times together, always, were on my mother's terms. She sent for me, no doubt, when she was feeling strongest, dismissed me when her strength or mood ran out. She controlled what I would recall.

So possibly I saw nothing. Or saw, but could not bring myself to know. The record is in the remembering: Our times were happy but few.

I imagined her as a queen or princess. Beautiful, aloof, mysterious, answering always to demands beyond my understanding, insulated behind servants and nannies who seemed to exist to do her will. Our moments together, rare and ritualized and always without my father, seemed secret to me, illicit almost. And the more cherished because of it.

I never questioned that she loved me, that she treasured our little rites as dearly as I did, or that she would have defended me, if she could have, against my father's rages. I knew that she feared him, just as I did, and never blamed her for her fear. I imagined that we shared an alliance, futile and unspoken but comforting in its complicity, of weakness against strength. I saw her weakness as my own. It was part of why I loved her.

My father could blow perfect smoke rings: one after the other, little staccato bursts of white that would form links of three, like the Ballantine Ale sign. It was his best trick, and no one else could match it.

I remember once, on a weekend night in our living room, watching them try: men and women in tweed coats and long dresses posted in all corners of the room, their mouths puckered into little o's, tapping their cheeks with their index fingers, trying to make the three-ring sign. At the end, with the room filled with smoke and everyone's mouth dry and stale-tasting, they all refilled their glasses and gathered around my father, who demonstrated—for the hundredth time—the technique behind his perfect rings.

"*The tongue,*" he said, sticking it out of his mouth and pointing. "*The tongue, the tongue*—it's the key to the whole thing."

But his trademark were the Jew jokes. These he told at nearly every gathering, always to gales of laughter. He had an endless supply of them; it seemed to renew itself from telling to telling, I never knew from where. And although there were some standbys, there was always enough new material to make for a good performance.

And they *were* performances: passionate, drawn out, nearly always delivered in exaggerated, singsong Jewish dialect. I thought they were wonderful—I had no idea why, beyond the funny voice and strange, contorted faces that went with them—and looked forward to them as keenly as the grown-ups.

I remember only fragments. There was one about the Columbia basketball team—my father had attended Columbia briefly and unsuccessfully years before, as a law student, and had viewed it ever since as a stronghold of what he termed the "Jew scourge." The joke involved him hopping around the floor jerkily in widening circles, like a penguin in galoshes, making grotesque faces, passing an imaginary ball between unseen opponents:

> *Ikie pass to Paulie,*
> *Paulie pass to Saul,*
> *Und dis de vay Colum-ski play*
> *de bis-ket-ball.*

There was another, a musical parody sung to the tune of "Good King Wensceslaus," which he performed faithfully every Christmas at my grandmother's. I've forgotten most of the words to this (no doubt because I never understood their humor to begin with), but they must have been clever, because although the song never changed from year to year, it always drew the same crowd to the same corner of my grandmother's living room.

"Archie's going to do Wensceslaus." The word would go out sometime after dinner, and at least half the adults, and some of the children, would scramble in to hear. My father would wait till everyone was present, then begin slowly, with great ceremony, picking up the tempo as he went, drawing laughter at every line: "Yonder Chreest-shun, voo is he? Ver und vot his *dvell*-ing?"

By the time he was finished, you could hear the howling three rooms away through closed doors.

It was always like that. He was the center of every room. On weekends at home, on summer nights at our camp in the Adirondacks, at my grandmother's on Christmas—if there was a crowd gathered and a bar nearby, my father would become a social machine. There seemed no limit to his skills: toasts, jokes, songs, smoke rings, stories, tricks, impersonations. His talents were magic to me. I practiced them privately in front of mirrors.

I wanted to *be* him—his voice, his laugh, his smell, his easy swagger. Even the fear he struck in me. I wanted to be that powerful, that sinister, that sure of who I was. I wanted everything he had. It was my earliest ambition. I measured myself in his glances.

"You're going to grow up as handsome as your father," the weekend ladies would tell me, plucking deviled eggs from my hors d'oeuvres tray and mussing my hair with a wickedness I grew quickly to like. "Lady-killer" is the word I remember. I was the "image" of my father: same mouth/nose/smile/high cheekbones. One of them told me once, at age seven, maybe eight, that I was "sexy."

I wanted badly to believe them. They were pretty, these ladies. They wore long, bright dresses, sometimes with low fronts, and smelled wonderful and laughed often through straight white teeth, and seemed to care about nothing so much as the hour ahead of them.

They spoke of secret things, too, things not meant for my ears, which they would spell sometimes in my presence (s-e-x was the only one I knew). Other things were referred to in broken French—words I couldn't understand but knew were dirty and forbidden and lay awake nights assigning meanings to. They winked and whispered to each other when I was in the room, smoked through cigarette holders, and sat in the laps of every man but their husband.

Often they pulled me onto *their* laps, where I would sit as they tweaked my cheeks and fed me tiny sips from the clear, bitter drinks they always kept refilling. I would sip, then wriggle and screw up my face—the same way I did from lemon or grapefruit—and the living room would howl in unison.

I *loved* these nights, though they rarely lasted long for me—half an hour, I suppose, or even less. The signal of their ending was always the same: Nanny in the doorway. All in white from neck to foot, as still as a statue, smiling slightly—a little cruelly, I thought—at the corners of her mouth. I never knew who had sent for her, or how she knew to come. A specter arriving. I dreaded the moment.

"One more time around with the tray, dear," my mother would tell me then. "Say good night to our guests."

On this last trip around, usually, I would get the quarters. From the men mostly. The women, the regulars anyway, gave me kisses. I went to bed smelling of Chanel.

My father was always last. Sitting in his chair in the corner by the fireplace, nearly always ringed by guests, he would reach up and feint a left or right to my stomach, catching me—every time—with the other hand to the side of my face. His hand was open, of course, and he always grinned when he did this, but it never didn't hurt.

"Keep your left high, old man, don't let me fake you. . . ."

Then he would slap me on the bottom, my mother would blow a kiss from across the room—and Nanny, who had never trailed me by more than a step in my final hors d'oeuvres tour (as though I might bolt for the door and sully her cameo), would remove the tray from my hands, smile serenely at my mother, and lead me from the room. The shame of this moment never lightened for all the times it was repeated.

Later in my bed—my room was the last one at the end of a long narrow hallway, across from my parents'—after Nanny had said good night and turned out my light (having read me, depending on which one she was, a chapter from *The Hardy Boys* or from the Bible), I would lie awake in the dark with the door open, often for hours, ingesting every sound:

Sometimes it was singing. Yale songs, campfire songs ("We are poor little lambs . . ."), with my father's voice always the loudest and surest ("who have gone astray . . ."), reaching me down the long hallway as if borne through a tube. Other times laughing: sharp, cracking guffaws that would come at the end of a minute or more of muffled buzzing. I imagined then that he had just finished a joke or story, that the living room was rocking with appreciation and applause—every eye wet with tears, the weekend ladies holding their sides to keep from splitting their flimsy bright dresses. I had seen it happen just this way, so many, many times. I was sure I had it right.

And from this knowledge came a certain comfort. I need not be there, I was a member already. I knew the patter—the jokes and stories, preambles and responses, the sound and tone and feel of those nights—as intimately as any regular. It was mine as much as theirs. I would claim it soon enough.

Of their life together I knew next to nothing. There was little for me to know. I could count on both hands, or nearly so, the times we were together as a family—only the three or four of us, with no guests or maids or nannies to diffuse the flow.

A scattering of Christmas mornings; a Yale hockey game with my half brother as star—my father screamed himself hoarse, and I swore to myself, if it was the last thing I did, I would learn to play hockey like that. Several fishing outings; a birthday lunch or dinner for my father at "21" (he poured Champagne into my water glass and told me to pretend it was ginger ale); some summer car trips to and from the Adirondacks. Few of these are happy memories. Some are worse than others.

I never thought of them as a couple. "My parents" would have been an impossible reach. They were "Daddy" and "Mummy"—the one vital and fearsome, a master of smoke rings, the other as fragile and lovely as a bird. Neither of these visions was closer than halfway to the truth—or even to the little bits of truth I'd seen—but they were close enough for me.

I knew, I must have known, that they despised each other. He wore his contempt for her like a badge in her presence: She was "Little Miss Priss," a "prig," a "goddamn whiner," once even in front of guests. As for her, her terror of him was as palpable as my own.

They fought, but rarely. More times than not, it wouldn't get that far. She would retreat after the first few forays, like a skulking dog. I remember her silences, her downcast eyes, the way she'd press herself against the inside of the car door for hours at a time, never looking up, hardly seeming to breathe, on those endless, awful trips to the Adirondacks.

I pitied her. I wanted to cry for her, to shake her and make her fight back—to fight back myself. But I knew my father's scorn, and the price of defiance, as personally as she did. Or so I thought. And so instead, usually, I pretended to be asleep.

I never saw him hit her, though I must have known he did. He hit *me*—sometimes with his belt in the name of "discipline," other times with his hands with no excuses offered—and her fear of him was a mirror of my own.

It wasn't something I thought about. I thought very little, when I thought at all: "Daddy has a temper, Mummy makes him mad." It was not a lie. And the small, simple truth it offered made further truths redundant. I was not blind, only careful not to see too much.

And in fairness, there wasn't much to see. The real horrors played out beyond my sight. What was left was a diorama: frozen in images of closed doors, muffled voices, the silence and secrecy of their comings and goings ("in Europe," "in Albany"), the two of them at opposite ends of the living room on weekend nights.

Beyond these things, and the tawdry, lonely lessons they taught, I remember only fragments. There is little to remember. We were a family only in name.

Two

I learned to tie a tie when I was five. My father showed me how, then made me practice without a mirror until I could make the wide end land flush with the top of my shorts, three times out of three. By the time I entered Buckley School, three months after my sixth birthday, I was a better tier than he was. He never admitted this to me—he would say only that my tying "made the grade"— but I studied his ties every chance I got and I knew that it was true.

Ties were part of the uniform at Buckley, as were (except in winter) blue or gray shorts with button-on suspenders, dark blue knee socks, brown oxfords, a white or blue shirt, and a dark blue cap with fold-in ear flaps and a silver *B* on the front. Dark blue was the Buckley color and, according to my father, nearly all of whose suits were blue, the one most "fitting for a gentleman."

He spoke often in such terms—of things being "fitting" or not fitting, of "making the grade," "measuring up," or "cutting the mustard"—as though life itself were some sort of diving meet or dog show, with points awarded or deducted for form and poise.

The ultimate standard, the gauge against which all things and people were judged, was something he called the "Gentleman's Code." This was never explained or defined, and seemed to embrace different things at different times. But the basics were clear to me before I ever tied my first tie.

A gentleman never cried, complained, or shied from a fight ("good guts"), always shook hands firmly and made eye contact ("good breeding"), stood and walked with shoulders back, never boasted or showed off, was mindful of his "good name," and—in my case at least—ideally spoke only when spoken to.

I was tested often on these tenets, and nearly as often failed. My handshake was never firm enough. I walked always in a "goddamn slouch." I flinched and hissed when iodine was applied to a knee or shin. My father once, taking the bottle out of Nanny's hands, poured half of it over a roller-skating cut. I managed somehow, that time, to remain dry-eyed and still.

"You got good guts," he told me—his exact words—and I carried his praise with me for a week.

Another time, as a second-grader, getting off the school bus in front of our building, I was set upon by a bully several years older and half again my size. He bloodied my nose, welted my forehead, and tore the buttons from my shirt. I was proud of my wounds and of my survival, but ashamed that I had not fought harder.

A minute later, alone on the landing outside our apartment and knowing that my father was home, I rubbed the knuckles of my right hand against the rough wall surface until I drew blood. Then I ripped what was left of my shirt, matted my hair over my forehead with spit and blood, and went inside to show him.

He asked if I had won. I told him no, but the other boy was much bigger, I had done well. He rang for the elevator, hauled me into it by the collar, and took me back out to the street. The boy was still there. My father told us he wanted a "fair fight," then ordered me to hit him. I did, or I tried to, the boy hit me back, and I fell and began crying. My father picked me up, held me on my feet, and screamed at me to fight. I kept crying, and the boy walked away. My father let me drop in a pile on the sidewalk and walked inside disgusted.

Still, he awed me. I worked endlessly to earn his praise. Like my mother, I saw him mostly in passing. But I knew well how busy and important he was: a state legislator, "in Albany, making laws." I came to believe that any time he gave me was more than he could spare, like a visitation with the Pope or President. A sacrifice. I coveted his minutes.

His district, the "Silk Stocking District," comprised much of the Upper East Side. Every second year, when he ran for reelection, the ten or twenty blocks that formed my world would be papered with his posters:

Archibald Douglas Jr.
Honest, Sincere, Conscientious
Has Served You Ably in Albany for Six [Eight, Ten] Years
Vote Row A All the Way

He was everywhere. Staring down at me from at least one building on every second block, fifty times life-size, or so it seemed. Stern, wise, implacable, handsome, important, a god. No other boy in the city, perhaps anywhere, had such a father.

"I remember campaigning for him," my younger sister says today. "I couldn't have been more than four or five. Nanny and I would go out together in the neighborhood with this stack of handbills he'd give us—me in this frilly little dress, my Lady Jane shoes, the perfect princess—and hand them out to people in the street, or put them on bus seats.

"It was exciting in a way. The human advertisement—'Could Any Little Girl This Cute Have Anything But a Prince for an Old Man?'

"I got the gist, even then. . . ."

My father was serious about his politics. They were, I think, the only religion he understood. It would be years before I saw this, though I learned early that his passions, at least the ones I witnessed, were often political.

Any mention of a Democrat, no matter how innocent, was unthinkable in his presence. (Years later, as a teenager, I would be sent from the table without dinner for suggesting that the New Deal might have had some merit.) Democrats were a subclass of the world's pariahs—"niggers," "kikes," "Reds," "frogs," "limeys," "mackerel-snappers"—all of whom, I knew from a young age, were the source of every evil I would ever know or experience.

There is a story in our family. It couldn't possibly be true, and like most stories, it grows a bit from telling to telling. Still, however impossible, it is a story that fits the man which, no doubt, is why it still occasionally gets told. It has survived now nearly fifty years.

My parents were hosting a party on a spring afternoon in 1945. The news arrived that Roosevelt was dead. After much whooping and toasting, it was noticed that my father had vanished. His guests looked everywhere for him, but he was not to be found. He had abandoned his own party, it seemed, without a word.

Half an hour later he appeared at the front door. It was April, and warm outside—he was wearing an overcoat, full-length and fully buttoned. It seemed to be sagging, the story goes.

He walked straight past his guests, toward the bedroom. My mother, fearing no doubt that he was sick or that the news of the President's death had unbalanced him, followed a minute or so behind.

The bedroom was vacant. The bathroom door was closed. She knocked—no answer. She opened the door.

And there was my father—as it is always told—squatting on the tile in front of the toilet, the overcoat still on him, "this shit-eating grin on his face."

From the side pockets, one by one, he pulled rolls of Roosevelt dimes. One by one he tore them open, dumped the dimes into the toilet—five dollars at a pop—and flushed.

He had a hundred dollars' worth. He didn't stop flushing, or smiling, until every one was gone. Then he returned, like a peacock, to his guests.

My mother, I'm told, used to love to tell that story. My father, I'm sure, loved hearing it. And if anyone dared remind them that Roosevelt dimes weren't even *minted* until the year after F.D.R.'s death, it has done nothing to dampen the myth.

I assume they're Republicans?" he asked me once, only half joking, of the family of a new friend. I was midway around the room, in pajamas and bathrobe, a plate of hors d'oeuvres in my hands.

"They *act* like Republicans," I replied, dead earnest.

He roared at this—everyone in the room roared—and thumped me on the back.

"Chip off the old block!" he said. He called me this a lot—when he wasn't calling me other things—and I learned in time to be grateful for the praise, though I rarely understood what I had done to deserve it.

I feared his anger as I've never feared anything, before or since. It came from nowhere—like his praise, like his moods—and attacked fiercely, sometimes violently, without warning. I know today that it hinged on how much rye he'd had, but at the time I knew only to be afraid.

Once, when I was seven or eight and the Korean War was an almost daily topic—being the creation, in my father's view, of "that jackass Truman"—I brought home a dancing school prize, a green fez hat with a red star on the front. My father was home alone, except for the servants.

I wore it proudly into the living room, displaying it, awaiting his praise. He liked it when I won things: races, fights, push-up contests at school, anything to do with strength or speed or manhood, anything that proved my mettle.

"There are boys *dying*!" he shrieked at me now, tearing the hat off my head and throwing me to the floor. "And you wear *that*? You wear *that*, in *my* home?"

He had me pinned to the floor, his knees across my shoulders, ranting about the Reds, when the front door opened behind him. It was George, our doorman, his arms full of shopping bags. My mother was a step or two behind.

George pulled him off me, then excused himself. My mother wept briefly before retreating to the bedroom. I went to the kitchen and cried in Bea's lap. It was never mentioned again.

There were kinder times. He could be soft, even tender, when it suited him. He pinched me on the butt sometimes when we passed in the hall and called me "Little Man." He mussed my hair, then combed it back, then mussed and combed again, explaining each time that "your part needs training."

Often, just before bedtime, he would take my younger sister out of Nanny's arms, perch her on his lap, stroke her hair and nuzzle her face and mutter, "Princess, princess, my little princess," so often and so absurdly that my mother and I would be making faces by the end. He was a sap. It was his harmless side.

I often woke in the night with leg cramps. They were painful but

not excruciating; left alone, I would fall back to sleep within minutes. Sometimes, though, especially during my first- and second-
grade years, when my mother was gone for weeks at a stretch ("in
Europe," I was told), my father would appear at my door late at
night with a glass in one hand and a bottle of rubbing alcohol in the
other, then sit at the end of my bed and talk and drink and rub my
calves—firmly, always from the ankles up—usually for longer than
it took the pain to go away.

I would try to tell him this: that it was all right to stop now, that
I was better and could go back to sleep—but he would keep on
talking and rubbing, pouring the alcohol into his cupped hands
before applying it to lessen the coldness against my skin.

I understood that he was lonely at these times—I never thought
it might be more than loneliness, or not loneliness at all—and that
he needed to talk and to share my company. I was glad to give it,
and grateful for his kindness.

He said my cramps were "growing pains," early proof of the
"good muscles" that would enable me, when the time came, to
win the Gordon Medal at St. Paul's—for "Best Athlete," an honor
my half brother, fifteen years older than I and a demigod of athletic achievement, had won already. I would not only never win it,
but would be thrown out of St. Paul's following my junior year,
breaking the chain of Douglas glory and staining the family honor
with what my father called a "stigma" that no future successes
could ever erase.

He talked often at these times of the "good name" I carried,
and of his plans for me: "You're bright, you'll go far." There was no
blessing in the world, he said, more precious than a good name.
It was a gift that others before me had earned, and I must prove
worthy of. He never spoke of how I should manage this (beyond
reminders of the Gentleman's Code) and it would be years before I
understood how or why I was so blessed. But I can't remember ever
not knowing it.

He was drunk, of course. But I knew nothing of drunkenness. What I knew was that the smell of my father was the smell of whiskey (Bellows Partner's Choice), that it was as much a signature of his presence as perfume of my mother's, and that both were badges of a world I wanted badly to join.

He disapproved of television. "Insanity in a box," he called it and swore it would never last. And so we had none. Radio was a different matter: "Gangbusters," "The Shadow," "The Lone Ranger," "Hopalong Cassidy," "Amos n' Andy," "Mr. Keene, Tracer of Lost Persons"—I could recite the lead-ins to every one.

My father liked some of them too. And from time to time, on nights when my mother was away, he would rescue me from Nanny after supper and we would listen together in the living room, usually to "The Shadow" or "Mr. Keene"—he in his chair in the corner by the fireplace and me across from him, the little Magnavox on the table between us.

These were the best times, the purest times, we ever shared. I can remember no speeches, chidings, or calls to manhood. We listened far more than we talked, and when we did talk, it was mostly to bet quarters on outcomes we both pretended not to know, then to curse or applaud the acts of guilty butlers and avenging, mysterious strangers with high-sounding names. ("Lamont Cranston, a man of wealth, a student of science, a master of other people's minds, devotes his life to righting wrongs. . . .")

Usually, at the end—with Nanny hovering behind us in the doorway like a giant white bird—my father would flip me, double or nothing, for the quarter I had nearly always won. Somehow, almost without fail, I went to bed with an even buck.

But this was all, or nearly all. He promised many times to take me to the Polo Grounds for a Giants game, but we never went and after a time I stopped believing we would. And it was my half brother, a visitor on weekends and holidays, who taught me how to ice-skate and throw a football. I learned to ride a bike from an uncle in Connecticut, and about sex from magazines and third-grade mischief. (From the school-bus window on the way down York Avenue: "Lady, lady, your bra is slipping!" "What's a bra, Jock?" "You don't know? It makes their *tits* bigger.")

He did teach me how to cast a fly and gut a trout, during our summers in the Adirondacks, and he was there when I caught my first fish, a fourteen-inch rainbow, in a shallow lake in the summer of 1950. (My mother, seeing my struggle, moved across the boat to help me. He screamed so loud I almost dropped the rod: "It's *his* fish!" I was grateful—that time—for his defense of my honor.)

Other than this, though—and tying a tie, and the importance of keeping my left held high—there are no skills worth knowing that I remember having learned from him. It would wound him deeply to hear me say this. He wanted badly to believe he was my mentor, and in darker, deeper ways he was. But the truth was too simple to make excuses for. I knew it about him, I think, as early as I knew anything: My father didn't like kids.

"Seen but not heard." The first idiom I ever truly understood, it carried the weight of a Commandment. Spoken always tonelessly—sometimes dangerously—and always with its subject understood, it was, I knew, the core mission of every nanny ever hired. One of them, a Miss Green whom we called Greenie, would recite it mindlessly several times a day, like some numb-brained acolyte, as grounds for every request denied or postponed: "Can I go to Kurt's house?" "Can we go to Reeses's?" . . . "Seen but not heard."

He hugged me often, as randomly as he hit me, for reasons probably neither of us knew. His hugs were clutching and desperate, and lasted far too long. I was embarrassed by them.

Once, driving back late at night from a picnic in the Adirondacks the summer I was seven—he had been singing bawdy songs around the fire, I'd been drinking orange sodas, awaiting our departure—he reached across the seat, without reason or warning, and pulled me to him, so fiercely I thought the car would leave the road.

"I'm so *proud* of you," he said huskily, his eyes all fervent and filmy. "So *goddamn* proud."

For the next minute or two, he drove shakily, his left hand on the wheel, his right arm pinning me to his side with such force I almost couldn't breathe. He was crying, his eyes so full of tears I wondered that he could see the road.

It was as though he were afraid of losing me. Or losing something, and I was all there was to hold. I was frightened for him—for us both, I guess—but too ashamed to say a word.

Halfway home he began to ease his grip, and before long his arm was limp around my shoulders, as though he'd forgotten it was there. Then he removed it altogether, and began singing—the same tunes he'd been singing all night. His tears had dried. The moment, it seemed, had never been.

Three

We lived on Fifty-seventh Street, as far east as you can go, the last awning before the river. "Sutton Place," my parents called it, and as fictions go it was easy to forgive. But the real Sutton Place began at the corner, and we were a hundred feet short. On such small colorings a whole world can be built.

New York was a cleaner city in those days, and the sidewalks near our home were cleaner still: policed free of riffraff, hosed and swept daily by doormen, planted here and there with scrawny, six-foot saplings circled at their base by little metal collars to keep the poodles from wetting on the roots.

Most of the buildings, like ours, were brown brick, while others were a faded red, but aside from this they were all nearly the same: fifteen stories more or less (we lived on the fifth), fronted by wide green awnings and heavy iron-and-glass doors. The lobbies were drafty and high-ceilinged, ringed usually by mirrors or somber-looking murals of ancient Chinese landscapes, dragons, and swordsmen on horseback. And sometimes, at intervals around the sides, lonely, red-silk backless sofas that only the doormen ever used.

There were doormen everywhere, especially on sunny days: hailing taxis, holding doors, balancing shopping bags for fur-wrapped ladies in dark hats who smiled crisply and never looked sideways. They all wore matching blue or green trousers, caps, and coats, the trousers with silver piping down the seams, the coats with bright brass buttons and, sometimes, epaulettes. Most, like ours, were gray-haired and jowly and looked like old soldiers. They waddled when they tried to run: on rainy days, scurrying outside with their broad green umbrellas to greet ladies debarking from taxis or private cars, offering their arms as leverage over puddles.

Our doormen, George and Pat—George was enormous and merry and smelled like cigars, Pat was red-faced and spoke with a brogue, which I loved—knew all the children in the building by name, and would play games with us in the mornings while we waited in the lobby for the school bus to come. (Most of the boys in the building went to Buckley or St. Bernard's, the girls to Chapin or Spence.) On weekend afternoons, when we arrived home with Nanny from the zoo or the museum or the little park across the street, Pat would tip the big blue cap he wore and ask if we had had a "jolly day." I thought of them as family, or nearly so, and made them drawings at Christmas and told them my secrets.

Our apartment was large, though probably not the cavern I remember: three bedrooms off a long narrow hallway that seemed always unlighted; living room and dining room in front, overlooking the street; and in back, off the service entrance, the kitchen, pantry, and maid's room.

The furniture was mostly heirloom hand-me-down: hinged mahogany end tables, poster beds with scrolled inlays, brass table lamps, a gilt-colored living-room rug that turned up at the edges. The walls were hung randomly with "sporting art"—nesting pheasants, a retriever in mid-stride—as if to create the spirit of a men's club or hunting lodge.

For myself, I remember no spirit at all, except a vague sense of things being dirty, which could hardly have been the case, so it may have been just the oldness of everything.

My parents, except on weekends, were rarely at home. Or rarely accessible, and there seemed to be no difference. We lived between Mondays and Fridays like squatters in a church.

There were only the four of us: my sister and I—she was three when I was seven, and good for little except to bully—Bea, who rarely came out of the kitchen, and Nanny, whoever she was at the time: German or Irish, mousy or haggard, stern or tender. We came and went, each of us, in our own narrow, prescribed orbits around the same little rituals at the same times of afternoon and night: playtime, wash-up, mealtime, bath, homework, story, bed.

The apartment shrunk itself to the meagerness of our days and needs. Parents' room off-limits, living room unused and forgotten. Bea and Nanny, curators to a world they could neither join nor fathom, knew their place and kept to it. As for us, we never mussed, shouted, scattered toys, wore old clothes, stayed up late, trick-or-treated, had a friend over, threw food, tracked mud, or went to bed without pajamas. Rarely have four people failed so utterly to fill a home.

"I think of it as the setting for every ghost story I've ever heard," my sister says today. "You know, the escaped-maniac stories, the bloody fingers on the bedpost. In my mind, they're all set in that apartment. The place was gothic—worse than gothic, *surreal.* Everything so big and still, the hallway so long, you could never hear anybody's footsteps, there were weird shadows. It scared me *so* much, I had dreams you wouldn't believe.

"There was a fly one afternoon in my room—I was supposed to be napping. Just a regular housefly, I could see it. Only the longer I lay there in bed, the bigger it got. It *grew* while I watched, like one of those flowers in kids' movies about plant growth, till it seemed like it was the size of a bat—or maybe it *was* a bat, I can't remember. And it was right over my head, right over the bed, this huge flying thing, buzzing and flapping its wings. . . .

"Finally I screamed. And Bea and Nanny came tearing in, both of them together, like a couple of firemen to the rescue. And when they figured out what the problem was, they got bedsheets—these two old women, flapping bedsheets at a housefly, yelling, 'Shoo-fly, Shoo-fly.' . . . I felt so powerful."

In my memory, it is always early evening there. The sky outside is dark or half-light, and in the wide gray building across the street with the circle driveway, the windows turn from black to yellow as I watch—randomly, in twos and threes, like clustered fireflies. A dull red glow from the neon Pepsi sign on the Queens shore mixes with the headlights; it will brighten as the darkness deepens. Below my window, a squat white stepvan with lettering that has always puzzled me—"OVER 40 YEARS FINK MEANS GOOD BREAD"— turns the corner from York Avenue and moves west into the city. It and the taxis are the only traffic. The sidewalks are empty. There are the sounds of horns through shut windows.

Inside, it is always the same. Bedtime will come soon, supper is just coming or just past. From the hallway outside my room there is the smell of new paint, and a light so forceless it stops at the door. My parents' door is closed, always: a white door with a glass knob in a painting of a hall without windows. There is nothing behind it but darkness.

Nanny is somewhere, tending my sister probably: an indifferent foreigner all in white and a little girl too young to matter. Bea is in her kitchen, half a minute's walk through empty rooms. The smells of her soups die in the hallway between us. There is the sound of water running—my sister's bath, or Nanny's—and now and then, like voices felt more than heard from distant rooms, the sigh-ing *whi-sssssh* of George's elevator as it passes our floor on its way down or up.

I imagine sometimes that I am on it, invisible: I would get off each night at a new floor, walk unseen—"The Shadow"—through all the apartments, above and below, and capture the secrets of a hundred lives.

I have many such imaginings, most of them fashioned from radio scripts to suit my longings. One evening when I was six or seven, a "Gangbusters" broadcast acquainted me with the workings of a kidnapping. The same night, on a purposefully tattered scrap of lined school paper, I penciled a note—*Help! 455 East 57th Street, Apartment 5A*—and threw it out my bedroom window.

A night and a day went by. My adventure was forgotten. The next evening, a Friday or Saturday, not long before my parents' guests were due, a pair of uniformed policemen arrived at our door, accom-panied by the building superintendent, who carried my note in his hand like an offering. He apologized for "the trouble"; the policemen seemed bored. My father, drink in hand and smelling of shaving soap, made small jokes about the "rubbish" in kids' heads, then marched me out to make amends. I said I was sorry, my father passed around his business card (it may have been a campaign flyer) and assured the men that there would be no more such nonsense. The door had no sooner closed than he threw me across the front hall. I passed no hors d'oeuvres that night, and ate supper in my room for a week.

I am in my room now, with my radio and my toys. Dump trucks that tip backward, police cars with sirens, army tanks and taxi cabs, pis-tols and rifles of all descriptions, a model destroyer with the gun tur-rets glued on backward; Golden Books, trading cards, Pez dispensers, baseball mitts, a chemistry set I have opened once and will never use.

My favorite is not a toy at all: a red leather pencil case stuffed with dollar bills I have collected from the weekend men or won in "bets" with my father. I recount the bills every night, arranging them by crispness in their case. There is nothing I am saving for—only the bulge of the case in my hand when I hold it. There is safety in that bulge.

But I don't touch my toys tonight, or count my bills, and the radio is off. Next to it, on the table by my bed, is an accidental still life. A pair of small, unremarkable things bought for fifteen cents at Mumphrey's on the corner—the first unsupervised purchase I have ever made. They are perfect. I have never before loved anything so completely: a My Friend Flicka comic book and a pack of grape gum.

On the cover of the comic, which has cost me a dime, a tall brown mare with flashing eyes rears on her hind legs and slaps at the air. Her mane is long and wild, and disappears off the end of the picture as though it might continue unfurling forever. There is desert in the background.

The gum is unopened, its package barely touched: five sticks in a dark purple wrapper with silver and white lettering—"Wrigley's Grape"—the corners as sharp and perfect as the corners of a book.

For this evening and the few that follow, the private wonder of these two little treasures—the comic at an angle to my radio, the gum placed perfectly, diagonally, on top, the light glinting off them at angles that change endlessly as I move—fills me with a peace that nothing can touch. School goes by in a blur; bath and supper and Bible-reading are threaded through with Flicka and my gum. I lie awake at night, feeling with my fingers their shape in the darkness on the table next to me.

For forty years after, more consciously than not, I will measure everything sacred—every true love, every perfect moment, every still water at dusk—by the glow of my bedside still life when I was seven. I don't know if this is wonderful or sad, if I am lucky to have such a benchmark or pitiable to need it. But I know that I would miss it terribly if it were gone.

It is supper now, six o'clock or a little after. My sister and I—she is four, I am nearly eight—sit alone in the dining room at a table large enough to seat twelve. (Nanny takes her meals in the pantry with Bea.) It is dark outside, or nearly so, and the light from the glass chandelier over the table casts itself drearily over two walls of bird prints. The door to the living room is open, but admits only darkness.

I sit at the head, in the chair with the buzzer—my mother's chair—which I am to ring between courses or to signal for more milk or pie. Eleanor is several seats away, nearly at the opposite end, out of range of flying food and napkin rings. We eat in silence, hurriedly, Eleanor pushing her food onto a spoon too large for her mouth with a silver Tiffany's pusher, a christening present she has used since she was old enough to feed herself. I tease her about this ruthlessly in private, though at the table, within earshot of the pantry, my mockings remain silent: cruel caricatures of four-year-old clumsiness with which I press her deftly to the edge of tears.

The rules are clear, and will remain in place for years, through a string of nannies: We are to empty our plates before I can ring for Bea, and if our voices can be heard through the pantry door, we will be sent from the table without dessert.

Among all the little rituals of our days, suppers are for me the most dreaded. And will seem, in remembrance, the most grotesque. A thousand meals without words or laughter, or a single pea uneaten.

There was one refuge from the deadness. To close the door behind you at the entrance to Bea's kitchen, with half an hour to spend. It was like walking into sunlight from a cave.

Our times there, Eleanor's and mine, were nearly always stolen: never just before or just after mealtimes, or on weekends or school nights with homework to do, or too close to bedtime with Nanny on the prowl. But we found our times. Late afternoons usually, with Nanny listening to soaps in the bedroom, or napping or taking her bath.

The kitchen would smell of the beginnings of our dinner: soup, fried onions, a meatloaf in the oven. And we would sit with Bea at the little table in the pantry and help her shell beans or peel potatoes—one of ours for every ten or twelve of hers—and talk about our worries and our days. I don't know how much she listened, but she had answers for everything.

Bea was black and jolly and huge-hearted, and as big as a house. Especially her breasts. They were the biggest breasts I had ever seen. They seemed to extend from her neck to her navel, and rolled like Jell-O when she walked.

Or when she laughed, which was practically all the time. It began with a crack, like a shot exploding, went to a bellow, and ended in a rasp. It took nothing at all to make her laugh. Sometimes, I think, she did it just because she wanted to—or needed to, like screaming on an empty lake to hear your echo. I'd *pay* to hear that laugh today.

But as wonderful as it was (and as wonderfully defiant, in that strange, dead house) the real treat were her belches. They were as loud as the laughs at least, if they weren't louder, and sounded more like moose calls than anything human.

They happened, she told Eleanor and me (before we grew old enough to doubt her wisdom), because of the "hot air" stored inside her bosom, "like a balloon." They could be triggered, she said, by pressing on her breasts, which she called by some wonderful nonsense name like "hagahs" or "geelgahs"—I wish I could remember.

This she proved to us every chance we gave her, which was nearly as often as we made it to her kitchen.

"Press your hagahs, Bea? Please? Just once?"

"One push, that's all. And don't be thumping on me now. I'm not no horse, y'know."

And we would push—Eleanor on one breast, me on the other—as you would push on a rubber raft to force the air out.

"BAAAAAA-*UMP*," would come the sound, as long as a foghorn and nearly as loud, and we would giggle and she would roar and the process would begin again: "Any more hot air in your hagahs, Bea?" "Well, maybe just one more bit."

I remember her husband, though only vaguely. His name was Sterling. He drove an ambulance, and would come by sometimes on his way from delivering patients to the hospital, and sit in the pantry and talk with us. He had short hair and a big belly, and wore a uniform of some sort. They lived in Brooklyn, which was all I knew of Brooklyn: It was the town where Bea lived.

Sterling died when I was eight or nine—in his forties, I suppose—and Bea was gone for a week or so, then came back to work and moved into the maid's room, which had been empty before that. It was as though a piece of furniture had been broken, removed for repairs, then returned to us and moved to a different place.

Bea was a symphony—of sounds and stories and eternal, waddling movement. She laughed and belched, and cooked and cleaned and spun tales: her mother's tribe in Africa, her twenty-six siblings, an illegitimate son—we swallowed them all. She dried our tears, soothed our fears, and ran interference with Nanny ("I'll speak to her just this once, but I don't make no promises").

She never, ever took sides—especially against my father, whom she adored and would have defended for ax murder. He called her "my favorite nigger"—always with his best smile—and she would roar and blush like a teenager: "Oh, Mistah Douglas, you always teasin'."

She was no saint. She played both ends, and we knew it—a secret in Bea's kitchen only sometimes remained that way—but we forgave her easily and without grudges. She was an ally. She listened, made us laugh, and gave comfort where she could. She loved us, I believe, and we loved her back. Final allegiances were not important.

Bea was with us eighteen years, through more maids, nannies, crises, and changed circumstances than she could ever possibly have recalled. She outlasted both my parents—my mother by ten years, my father by one—and was finally retired, in the mid-sixties, by my widowed stepmother, on an annuity I once heard was five thousand dollars a year.

However much or little, it was enough, together with whatever she had saved, to meet her needs in a two-room apartment in the Williamsburg section of Brooklyn, where I went to visit her, with my sister, in the spring of 1970.

It had been years since I'd seen her. She had aged well. She was still vigorous, her step was just as quick. But there was a listlessness now, an air of defeat, that hung off her presence like a smell.

She introduced us to her best—perhaps her only—friend, her landlady, who had aquamarine hair and lived downstairs. We offered to take her out for lunch, but she wouldn't hear of it.

"I am a Neegruh-person. White gentlemen and ladies don't go out in public with Neegruhs. You should know that by now."

She was right. I should have known. For eighteen years, she'd been my father's pet nigger. For a lifetime, quietly, she'd borne her race like a cross. And now here I was—my father's son, telling her to throw it all aside for a trip to lunch. I should have known better. But I didn't. I felt rebuffed.

She made us lunch instead, the first meal she'd cooked for me in nearly eight years, and the last one she ever would. I don't remember what we ate, only that it was a difficult two hours. We were adults by then, at least in her eyes, and needed no ministering—and yet we were in her home. It confused her, I think. She was quiet, and hardly laughed at all. We left abruptly after lunch, with some excuse, and she made no move to keep us. We promised to return, but of course we never did.

I heard the news a year or two later, months after it happened. She'd been found on a street corner several blocks from her home, dead of a diabetic coma. No one had seen her collapse; it was hours before they'd found the body.

For nearly as long as I'd known her, Bea had given herself insulin shots every morning. Her only real fear, she'd told my sister once, was dying alone.

My world, bounded by Fifth Avenue, the river, and the perfect symmetry of my father's codes, was as chaste and well-ordered as a store window. I remember every corner in it:

The blocks and blankets in my nursery-school homeroom, the smell of Mrs. Chapin's perfume at DeRahm's Dancing School, where I was sent at six to learn the waltz and fox-trot and the rudiments of what Mr. DeRahm called "the social graces." The old man in Central Park who tied the knots on helium balloons (one hand, no string, faster than you could say "rhinoceros"); Radio City and Ringling Brothers; G.I. Joe trading cards during the Korean War. The smell of bread from the factory on the East River Drive. The sandbox in the little park on Fifty-seventh Street where we went with Nanny before I was old enough to roller-skate.

The sandbox *was* the park. There were no swings or bars there, nothing to climb on or hang from. The red-brick flooring was too rough for roller skates. There was only the sandbox. It sat in the middle, a small sunken trough, the center of a square whose sides were the river and the nannies' benches. For five hundred afternoons at least, before Buckley claimed my weekdays and my first pair of roller skates took me—on weekends—to the big boys' park uptown, that sandbox was kingdom to the shapings of my world.

I built fortresses, defending them with platoons of cowboy-soldiers; collapsed tunnels on the cars and trucks of other boys and girls. I built nothing well. I was not a builder. I peopled, defended, and destroyed. For most of those days, I ruled the sandbox. When I could not rule, I protested, cried, then ran for help.

The nannies' benches were the tribunal to which we went for justice: "Geoffrey smashed my dump truck," "His dump truck flattened my fort."

They dispensed it dully and with menace—"You want the hairbrush when we get home?"—then went back to their chatters. We slunk away unresolved.

They chattered endlessly, sometimes a dozen at a time. Wizened, white-linen harpies with down-turned mouths for whom shrillness seemed the only goal: past lives, past jobs, the slovenliness of their wretched little charges, the shiftless indifference of the Sutton Place mothers who signed their checks.

If the exchanges of a single hour on those benches could have reached the ears of their employers, not a nanny among them would have kept her job.

Other parks came later, with other children: roller skates, jungle gyms, swings with safety bars, then with none. Hopscotch and tennis-tag. The tyranny of a new nanny who revoked the privileges of the old. I carry them with me like an album in my mind.

But such a thin, bowdlerized little album. Snapshots from a doll's house. I knew, vaguely, that Harlem was peopled by Negroes; I felt more shock than pity at the old man with the shriveled face who sat outside Bloomingdale's before Christmas every year. I had seen once, from the window of a taxi, two teenagers pummel an old man, break his cane on the side of a building, then run away with the bag he'd been carrying. But I might as well have been staring through a prism at the moon.

Once, at the zoo in Central Park when I was six or seven, a black boy tore a balloon from my hand, burst it on the ground, leered, spat at my feet, and ran away. I was furious but confused. Why? I asked Nanny. I had done nothing to him. She took me by the hand, marched me to the monkey cage, and pointed:

"Negro people come from the monkey. They are stupid and dirty, they can't help what they do. But they are dangerous, and full of germs. You should never go near them."

I believed her. And thus began a nightmare that persisted for months, with variations: a troop of black people, men and boys, chasing me through a labyrinth in the dark, where they would finally corner me, smother me with their stink, then eat me piece by piece, beginning with my lips and nose.

Several years later, as a fourth-grader at Buckley, I was seen cheating on a test by a boy who sat in the row behind me. The boy, who was overweight and wore glasses and probably would never cheat on anything in his life, informed me at recess that he planned to tell the teacher. I begged him not to; I offered him my Pez dispenser and all the candies in it. He took the bribe and walked away.

Later that day, I was summoned to the headmaster's office, where I was told that a note had been mailed to my parents. If the incident were repeated, I would be dismissed from the school. Buckley did not abide cheaters.

I cornered the boy after school on the street, but he had made it to his bus before I could reach him. I couldn't follow.

"Jew! Jew! Dirty lousy kike-Jew!" I yelled at him, running along-side, as the bus pulled away. It was the worst insult I could think of.

I was my father's son. Years before the Jew incident, probably before I entered first grade, I understood, at least murkily, the make-up of the world. It was divided, I knew, into two uneven groups: The Good Names and the others. The Good Names—family, friends, schoolmates, the neighborhood—were smarter, handsomer, luckier in life, inexplicably transcendent. (Money wasn't part of the picture; I suppose it was assumed.) We knew one another instantly on sight, as if by code rings or secret signs. We were members of a club.

The others—teachers, nannies, maids, doormen, policemen, waiters, construction workers, beggars, Catholics, Democrats, nig-

gers, and kikes, in roughly descending order—ran the scale of infe-
riority from unenlightened to downright evil. Those near the top
end were to be tolerated, cultivated when necessary, and treated
always with courtesy. But also with reserve. Those at the bottom
were to be detoured at almost any cost. But without ruckus, in the
fashion of a gentleman, as you would sidestep a dog's business in
the street.

This lesson was never spoken, and I could point to no single
moment when it first shone clear for me. But by six or seven, I
think, I had digested its basics.

And it wasn't long after that I understood its corollary: that the
name I shared with my father was a door against the world, and the
worst thing I would ever have to fear was letting it open.

Years later, on an August afternoon in 1962, as an eighteen-year-
old recruit at Lackland Air Force Base in San Antonio—it was "Yale
or the service for any son of mine," my father had said, and Yale had
turned me down—I had drilled and run laps on a macadam parade
field almost to the point of dropping. It was over a hundred degrees
with no shade; my canteen had been empty for an hour. The recruit
next to me—he was black, and from Harlem—offered me a drink
from his. Before that summer, I had never known a black who
didn't work in a white man's yard or kitchen.

I stared at the canteen, for what must have been ten seconds,
before I took it, touched it to my lips, and gagged.

"Got a problem?" he asked.

"Sick," I said. "Sun's made me sick."

"Better take a drink then, man," he said. And I did, and gagged
again.

In the end, I was more thirsty than revolted. The third or fourth
swallow stayed down. And I knew, even then, that something
important had happened.

Four

At a little after two in the afternoon on the last Saturday of September 1953, two days before the start of my fourth-grade year, the day before the clocks went back for winter, I took the paper to my mother's room and found her dead.

I know the time because I looked it up, years later, on microfilm at the library. The day, too. I had remembered it always as a Sunday, the day of the thick *Herald Tribune* and color comics, the day we read and talked the longest, and made bets on next week's sequels. But it was a Saturday, so the paper must have been thin.

My father wasn't home. He hadn't lived with us since June. My mother had been out the night before. I'd recited her mnemonic in their bedroom, then watched her leave: carrying her night purse, walking away from me down the long hallway toward the door, a little before my bedtime. She had come home, I would learn later, sometime after midnight. It would be more than thirty years before I would learn where she had been or with whom.

She seemed to have been drinking, the night doorman would tell the police. Her eyes, he said, were red from crying. They had not spoken. He was the last to see her alive.

Noon passed, then one and two, and Bea's buzzer hadn't rung. I must have been impatient; I may have asked Bea to wake her for me, and been told she needed her sleep.

Sometime after two, furtively, I took the paper from its place on the table in the front hall and walked with it to the door of my parents' room. I must have felt, considering the hour, that my mother would be grateful to be woken, that she'd welcome me and we'd share Dick Tracy. Perhaps something similar had happened, on some earlier weekend, to give me this confidence.

I probably knocked. I know I went in. Beyond that, all memory stops: what I saw, what I did or thought, how long I stayed. Except that I knew, by the time I left the room, that she was dead—whatever that may have meant to me. I shed no tears, I made no scene, I don't know if I was scared or sad.

I met Bea in the hallway on the way out. I lied, claiming I had only knocked but not gone in. She scolded me briefly, went in herself, and came out running. It was then that, as the papers would report the next day, "the body was discovered by a maid."

After that I remember only chaos. My sister and I were told our mother was sick, dressed in a rush and taken to the park, and afterward to a toy store. We were gone until late afternoon. Sometime before we left, unable to contain my secret, I shared it with Eleanor, who was five at the time. She remembers this. I don't.

"We were sitting on the edge of the bed in my room, facing the hall. You were crying. You said Mummy was dead, that you'd found her body. I started crying—because *you* were, probably.

"I don't think I grieved much, I was pretty young. I hardly remember her at all—just this sort of dark presence, dark hair, dark eyes, and that she smelled good. Not much else. I can't say her death came as much of a blow. It was sort of exciting, actually. 'My mother is dead'—kind of heroic, you know?"

I was no less swept up in the drama of it. Sometime during our time at the park, I shared my secret for a second time, with a boy on roller skates, making him swear—"on God and the Bible"— he'd never tell. It is only because I recall doing this that I know today what I must have known then.

There were police everywhere when we returned. On the sidewalk, in the lobby, in our living room and hall. There was one posted at my bedroom door. Several months before, on a street corner on Third Avenue, I had seen police disperse a rally in defense of the Rosenbergs; for weeks after she died, I worried that my mother had been a spy.

The death certificate lists "acute barbiturate poisoning" as the cause of her death, with "mental depression" noted separately under the heading of "significant conditions." On the same document, in a multiple-choice section listing contributing circumstances, the option of "suicide" is crossed out in pen, as are "natural causes," "accident," and "homicide."

This leaves, by elimination, a single remaining choice: "undetermined circumstances pending further investigation." Such was the finding of Thomas A. Gonzalez, chief medical examiner of the City of New York, who signed the certificate on September 28, two days after my mother's death.

The "investigation" lasted two hours and forty-five minutes by official estimate. It took place that same afternoon, while we were at the park with Nanny, and consisted, I would learn later, of a cursory examination of her body ("the stiff in 5A," a policeman would call it, as he shared an elevator with my mother's sister) and brief interviews with Bea and the night doorman.

There was never an autopsy. My father, I'm told, used his

influence to prevent it. The police report, signed by Detective William J. Murdy of the 17th Precinct, makes no mention of a cause of death.

"Elinore [sic] Douglas found dead in her residence by maid . . . pronounced DOA by Dr. Peckman of City Hospital. Husband Archibald Douglas, Jr. present and ntfd. Body released this date to family by M.E. Gonzalez. Nothing suspicious. Case closed."

The New York tabloids, with few facts to burden them, wove clever little webs of uncertainty and innuendo—helped along by error and omission—then dropped the story for lack of fresh material. The New York *Daily News,* Sunday, September 27, 1953:

WIFE OF BLUE STOCKING LEGISLATOR FOUND DEAD

Eleanor Douglas, 38, wife of socialite Assemblyman Archibald Douglas Jr. of the 8th A.D., was found dead in her bed at 2:45 yesterday afternoon in the family apartment at 455 East 57th Street.

She had been under a doctor's care for several weeks, police said, and there were several medicine bottles—one of which contained a single pill—on a table beside the bed. Pending a medical examiner's findings, the case was listed as "open," but police said there was no indication that death resulted from other than natural causes.

The body, clad in a nightgown, was discovered by a maid. None of the rest of the family was at home. Douglas was at his club with friends, and the two children, Geoffrey, 9, and Eleanor, 5, were in Central Park. . . .

The night of the day she died we moved uptown to my grandmother's, where we would stay nearly two weeks, while our apartment was purged of memories and the marriage bed/deathbed replaced.

Granny's doorbell never stopped ringing. Aunts and uncles and cousins, brimming with hugs and small kindnesses, came and went in shifts. The only bed left for me was in a maid's room off the pantry. I cried every night we were there, and got lots of tenderness, most of it from Nanny, who was wonderful to me those weeks.

One night, in some clumsy tribute to my mother's memory, I dumped every gun I'd brought with me—six-shooters, cap pistols, ray guns, a G.I. Joe machine gun that spat sparks from its barrel— eight stories down the air shaft outside my window, listening to them smash and splinter on the cement below. I felt better instantly. My mother had hated guns.

My father was a wreck. It wasn't until our second day at Granny's that he could bring himself to tell me, formally, what I had known before he had.

"Your mother has gone to a better place."

We were alone in the living room, the double doors shut behind us. It was very still. My father was sitting on the arm of a chair, hunched over like a man about to vomit. He was shaking, his eyes so red it hurt to look at them. He was probably drunk. But his eyes never left mine. He was trying to be strong, trying his best to be a father.

"She's dead?"

"She's in peace now. She's happy where she is."

I knew, vaguely, that he was talking about God: the first and last such reference, in eighteen years of knowing him, I would ever hear him make. I was confused, and felt pandered to.

"I knew she was dead," I said. I wanted to make him say the word—*dead*—but he wouldn't.

I asked him if he'd told my sister.

"She said she hoped her mummy would have a good time in heaven."

At this he broke—noisy, guttural sobs that spasmed his body like punches landing. They passed, and he wept quietly, his head in his hands, without shame or restraint, for perhaps another half-minute. For the first time, I couldn't see his eyes.

"She loved you," he said.

I wanted badly to hug him, but I didn't. I don't know why. I would wish later that I had.

My half brother was waiting in the hall outside, bearing gifts: an Indian-bead belt with multicolored beads and some smaller thing I've since forgotten. Jimmy was nineteen, ten years older than me, my father's second son by his first marriage. A tall, stringy Yale sophomore with pale skin and close-cut hair, he had a girlfriend named Mary who was dark and pretty and called me her "yellow-bellied sapsucker." It was Jimmy who'd taught me how to throw a spiral, and had picked me up—fifty, a hundred times—off the ice at the rink at Rockefeller Center the first day I'd been on skates.

"Anywhere you want to go," he said. "Taxi's waiting, just say the word."

"Times Square," I said. "The arcades."

It was the closest thing I knew to heaven: skee-ball, table-hockey, shooting galleries, newspaper headlines you wrote yourself, rows of prizes you picked off shelves with coupons that were a cinch to win.

On our way downtown in the taxi, my brother told me he thought I was "holding up well." "Like a man," he said. "I'm proud of you. It's tough. I thought you'd take it harder."

He was trying to be a good brother. I was grateful, and tried back. "Don't worry about me," I told him. "I can take it."

For what must have been three hours, we shot ducks, whacked pucks, rolled balls into holes, dug prizes out of glass boxes with miniature steam shovels, stared cross-eyed together in picture booths, tested our grips on the "Strength-o-meter" (Jimmy ranked as "Superman"; I got "90-pound Weakling" till he put his hand over mine and raised it to "Lumberjack"). Skee-ball alone accounted for at least an hour. We played two lanes at a time, racking up coupons faster than we could track them. By the time we moved on to the Strength-o-meter, we had won enough to qualify for some serious booty: a collapsible telescope, a New York Giants baseball cap, a glass mug with the words "Times Square, New York, USA" in silver lettering around the sides. I took the mug with me a year later when I went away to school.

I don't know how many nickels my brother spent, but it must have been hundreds. They were well spent, though. Never once, from the moment we got there until half an hour before we left, did I think, even fleetingly, of my mother. It might have been the most fun I'd ever had. Jimmy saw this, I guess, and kept on spending. We stayed and stayed. I loved him for it.

The end came strangely. It was late in the afternoon. He was changing dollars for nickels, for the tenth or twelfth time, at the metal cage in the center. A red-haired woman in a bright dress, blood-red lipstick, and the highest heels I'd ever seen was standing behind him in line.

"That your father?" she asked me.

"No," I said. "My brother. Half brother, actually."

"Well, he's cute, whoever he is. Tell him for me I said he's cute, okay?"

I told him. He wasn't flattered.

"You don't want to talk to women like that," he said. His voice was cold. The woman was standing six feet away, smiling goofily at us. Jimmy steered me to the next aisle.

"If they try to talk to you, just walk away. Don't be rude, just walk away. They're bad news."

"Why? All's she said was that you're cute."

"You'll understand one day. Just don't talk to them, okay?"

He seemed angry—at me, at the woman, I couldn't tell which, but it almost didn't matter. I had no idea what had happened, why the woman was "bad news," or what it was that I was too young to understand. I knew, though, that something had been broken between us. I started to cry, then stopped.

"What's the matter?"

"Nothing."

"That woman scare you?"

"No."

"What, then?"

"She looks like Mummy."

It was a lie and I knew it, but it felt exactly like the truth.

My mother was buried in Yonkers the Tuesday after she died. I was at a movie with Nanny—a Western with Jimmy Stewart at the Fifty-seventh Street Loews—and didn't know until later that it had happened.

I threw a fit in Granny's living room. I wouldn't stop crying, I swore to my father, until he promised to take me to where she was. He was kind but firm, and very brief. It was out of the question, he said. It would only upset me more.

"And there's nothing to see but a stone."

The following Monday I returned to school. I had missed a week. There was almost no one who didn't know why. The headmaster, a small, serious man with a shiny bald head whose smile was indistinguishable from his frown, called me to his office my first morning back.

He was kind. He had been fond of my mother, he said (I hadn't known he knew her), and understood what a loss this must be. I shouldn't worry about the work I'd missed, he'd instructed the teachers to be lenient. I should carry his sympathies back to my father, and not hesitate to come to him if there was anything he could do.

"A Buckley boy's loss is Buckley's loss as well," he concluded, and sent me off to class.

I was a hero, the only half-orphan in my homeroom. The other boys treated me variously—with awe, pity, or indifference. But I saw only the awe.

I'd been given a photo of my mother: from the shoulders up, half smiling, beauty spot in place. It was black and white, wallet-sized. I owned no wallet, but kept it with me always: at school in my book bag, at home by my bed. My first week back at Buckley, I showed it to any boy who'd look at it: My Dead Mother. The Real Thing. It exalted my stature. By the time I'd been back a week, the corners were curled from wear.

"She was *pretty,*" one of the awed ones said to me one afternoon in the locker room. "Dead. Wow."

"I'll trade you," I said. I'd never meant to say it. The thought hadn't crossed my mind.

"For what?"

"Your Duke Snider. The autographed one."

The trade went down in the library between classes. My mother for Duke Snider—unsigned photo for autographed card, dead princess for live Duke. And for the first half-hour I reveled in my savvy.

Snider was a coup. One of the three big bats, with Robinson and Furillo, behind the great Dodgers teams of the late forties and fifties (six pennants in ten years), he would lead the league in homers three years later, finish twenty-first on the all-time home-run list, and wind up in the Hall of Fame. Only Mantle or Berra could have thrilled me more.

Word traveled. "You traded your mother's *picture?*" I heard it first in the gym playing dodgeball, then again later in class. By the end of the day it was the talk of the fourth grade.

"Who'd trade their mother's picture? She's *dead.* Wow, don't you even *care?*"

46

I was crushed. A traitor exposed. But the boy wouldn't trade me back. I went to a teacher, who went to the headmaster, who phoned my father at home. It was impossible, he told me when I got there, to trust me with anything. The photo was retrieved, then confiscated. I wouldn't see it again for a year.

We moved back home. The changes were everywhere. Small, sometimes hardly noticeable, but sinister somehow in the differences they implied. Like the first tiny furrows in a face that will grow monstrous with age.

My father's new bed was postless, the dressing table had disappeared. In the living room and hall, odd, irregular patches of bleachlessness spotted the walls where my mother's pictures had hung. Her writing desk had vanished, too: a cherry-wood slant-top with dainty brass fittings, replaced by a bulky off-green loveseat I had never seen. On the mantel over the fireplace, the books and figures had been disarranged; I couldn't be sure just how.

Other things, too. A new nanny came, then left, within weeks, then another after her. I barely learned their names. Bea hardly spoke anymore. Mirthless and dull-eyed, she went about her duties deep inside some private tent I could only guess at: a comrade, lobotomized. Her laughs, her belches, our history, seemed annulled. Even the doormen, George and Pat, gone somber and pious in their sympathies ("a fine woman, your mum, always a kind word for everyone, yessir, a real tragedy").

I wanted to shake them all—to reorder the world as I'd known it, dismal and too silent, but familiar in its patterns, with pockets of luster I'd learned long ago to bank on, like the quarters from the weekend men who never came anymore.

My father, for weeks, almost never left his chair. Days and nights, by the fireplace in his bathrobe—different patterns, always paisley,

47

always silk—reading his paper, refilling his glass. He was kind to me those months: hugs, ass-pats, sad-eyed smiles as I walked through or passed by. I saw his loneliness—or what I saw as his loneliness—and shared mine with him. We both gave, and got, some comfort.

We listened often to "Mr. Keene," but it was nothing like before. More rite now than pastime. He almost never bet me anymore, but his dollars had never been freer. My pencil case was fat.

My mother, as a subject, was off-limits. For all of us. No references, no memories, no mentions of her name. This was never stated as a rule, but I came to see it as one, and to respect the wisdoms I assumed were behind it: Time heals all wounds; the dead, being dead, are best forgotten.

I understood all this perfectly, tried my hardest to forget her, and waited—with my father, I supposed—for the loneliness to lift.

Only once, in the fifteen months we lived there after she died, did I hear her name mentioned. It was near the beginning, by Bea in the kitchen. I've forgotten the context, but the message fixed an image that stayed with me for years:

"She was smiling when I found her. A little smile, like from a happy dream. I knew, though, right away I knew. Her watch had stopped—it was still on her wrist, you know. Quarter to four, that's what time she died. You die with your watch on, it stops when your heart does."

Eight months passed this way, more or less. And then one afternoon, without a shadow of warning, there was a change. Or at least the promise of one.

"Wonderful news," my father said. He'd come to my room to tell me.

I asked him what. I guessed he'd won another election. He won so many, and they were so frequent, I thought for a moment I'd missed one.

"Mrs. Coe and I are going to be married."

"You're kidding," I said.

"Would I *kid* about something like that?"

"Why?"

"Because we want to, we love each other. We've talked about it."

"What about Mr. Coe?"

"They aren't married anymore."

"But *why?*"

"You'll have a mother again."

We talked some more. I said okay, and meant it. Mrs. Coe was my favorite of the weekend ladies. She wore long bright dresses with low fronts, and heavy gold bracelets that jangled when she shook her wrists. I liked her, and she could speak pig Latin.

My own mother, it seemed, had never been. Or had been, then passed from us without a trace: "Nothing suspicious. Case closed." A stone sunk without a ripple.

I was nine when she died, ten when my father remarried. I would be sixteen before I learned—by accident, through a family friend with too much gin in him—that she'd taken her life, and past forty before I knew of all the miseries that drove her to it. Thirty-five years of truths unraveling.

They are sad truths, most of them. A few are worse than sad. But sad or shocking or in between, they are the truths of more than one wrecked family or two wasted lives. They did not begin with my parents' marriage, or stop at its outskirts, or end when my mother died.

They are the truths of birth and breeding, of money and its echoes, of seeds planted where graves are dug.

They are history without modesty, through a mirror that should be a lens.

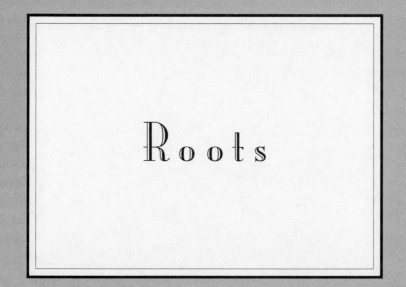

Roots

Five

A thick sense of time knits together the lines of those who came before us and those who come after us, our own boys and girls. But in the process time itself slows down, stifling opportunity and the grasp of opportunity, changing history from a one-directional progress to a series of spirals....

—*Old Money* by Nelson W. Aldrich, Jr.*

I never knew my grandfathers. One of them, my father's father, died eight months before my birth, the other a year after it. They were ciphers to me: no portraits on the wall, no remembrances recounted, not so much as a reference I can recall. I'm not sure, as a child, I even knew their names.

My grandmothers, I must have assumed, had been widowed forever. The younger of them, my mother's mother, was addled and frail by the time I remember her, and dying slowly of diabetes. I don't recall ever seeing her outside the hospital, where I went to visit her on Sunday afternoons, with Nanny and my sister. She gave me a dollar bill on every visit, rambled on endlessly about things and people I had never heard of, and frightened me with her feebleness. She died eight weeks to the day after my mother.

Granny Douglas frightened me too sometimes, but not because she was feeble. Anything but. She was near eighty by the time I remember her, the tiniest woman I had ever known (barely five feet tall in heels), seven-eighths blind and three-quarters deaf—but she could freeze you in place with a glance. She was a Lady. This, I think, was the first thing I ever knew about her, and the most important.

Her fingers were gnarled and crooked and as skinny as fish bones, and there were rings on several of them: gold, emerald, diamond, antique silver. She wore scarab bracelets and alligator shoes. Her hair was dyed gold-red and wrapped in swaths behind her head. I saw it unwrapped only once—on a pillow, a week or so before her death—and it was as thick and long as a girl's.

A cigarette grew out of her hand. It was Turkish, I think, or Egyptian, and smelled like incense. She *held* it really, more than smoked it, forgetting sometimes that it was there. The ash would droop impossibly, trembling like a faucet drip, until you rescued it for her at the last second, maneuvering the ashtray under it just in time to catch its fall. When Granny got up from her place on the couch, the ashes fell from her lap like sand off a child.

She would have made the perfect empress. She commanded just by looking. And when she spoke to you—whispered really, you had to bend your ear to her mouth to hear—she expected a reply. And not a lazy one. You didn't slide by with Granny, and you didn't make allowances, except to shout when you spoke to her, and to catch her ashes.

She was rich. Richer by far than we were, though not nearly as rich as her father had been. Her apartment, on Fifth Avenue overlooking the park, smelled of gardenia perfume and Turkish tobacco. The lushest smell I knew, I ascribed it to every princess, queen, palace, and castle I had ever heard of or read about.

The apartment was like a museum to me, only warmer and more festive. There was a sense of time and care, of elegance labored for—nurtured, pruned, and treasured—that was as absent from our home as sober laughter. Persian rugs, polished mahogany, Egyptian busts with eyes that followed you, Japanese screens of wonderful, stylized blue and red birds; framed lithographs, a musty, shelf-long collection of *Vanity Fair,* Maude Earl oils of ring-necked pheasant and blue herons perched over green water. You felt bathed in the richness.

Afternoon tea was a ritual with Granny, and all of her grandchildren—I was one of twelve—individually and at intervals, were invited to share it. It was tedious, but, like everything about her, sublime in its perfections: served in stages on silver trays, always in the library, with Jean or Delia—two of Granny's staff of four house servants, augmented by a chauffeur and secretary—arriving and departing endlessly with fresh plates of fruitcake and pots of tea and juice.

As often as not, there were other guests. Fellow matrons, hospital board members, the occasional artist or minor ambassador. Manners were at a premium.

Still, unlike at home, children were encouraged to take part. Questions on school, family, and friends were part of the process; responses were to be animated and pertinent, though never too lengthy. Even on adult subjects—business, politics, the war in Korea—our perspectives were welcome, so long as there was no silliness. You didn't clown or giggle at Granny's teas; you didn't bounce on knees or get passed around for kisses. You were an equal, or nearly so, and expected to behave like one. It may be that I learned more of the skills of my father's precious code in Granny's library than in five years of hors d'oeuvres–passing.

But when I think today of that apartment—when any of us remember Granny's, I suppose—I think first of Christmas evenings.

There were many of them. I went to my first at three years old, and never missed one until the last, when I was twenty, the winter before she died. I was probably a teenager before "party" ever conjured anything for me so vividly as Granny's Christmases.

There's no accounting really for why they were so special, or remain so treasured. They were family-only. All Douglases, or Douglases-by-marriage, or (on at least one—scandalous—occasion, when an older cousin was engaged to a Radio City Rockette) Douglases-to-be. They rarely varied, even slightly, except in the number of guests, which ranged between thirty and fifty.

The same handful told the same jokes and gave the same toasts, year to year. The menu always began with consommé and ended with pie. My father always drank too much, and Granny, nearly always, fell asleep before the end, sometimes at the table.

Part of it, I think, was the tradition itself. Our sense of a gilded, cocooned continuum, of children growing and elders aging against the static backdrop of Turkish ovals, British bird paintings, and French Champagne.

When I remember those Christmases, I remember them all as one: Granny ageless and in black, my father with no particular wife, my cousins in petticoats that blur quickly to evening dresses. It is a frozen portrait, one that ignores time and calamity and the meanness of some of our lives. All that mattered, then or now, were the certainty and the grace.

Dinner was the focus, though seldom the high point. (The Jew jokes came later, with brandy in the living room; and for the children, table hockey and filched Champagne.) At a single, oval table draped in white that stretched nearly the length of the dining room—the longest table I had ever seen, and the largest dining room—it was festive but controlled, like a well-run circus. We ate and drank and talked and laughed and toasted, and wore funny, pointed paper hats, and blew on cardboard noisemakers that were set at every place, and pulled ribbons from the favor-tray in the center. There was a ribbon and a favor for every diner, and your hat was never the same color as the hat to your left or right.

And all the while, Jean and Delia, in black with white aprons, and Hugh the butler, all in black, floated like ghosts around us—and the glasses kept refilling, the finger bowls disappeared, there were plates of lamb and mint sauce and sweet potatoes, then salad, then pie and coffee, then nothing but Champagne. It was a flawless, disciplined dance, full of noise and color and gaiety and the shared, simple pleasure of privilege as a bond.

Granny sat at the far end of the table, away from the kitchen, with my father—toastmaster and eldest son—always at the other. Between them on both sides, seated meticulously by sex, age, and affinity, with little mistletoed place cards to mark each spot, were an arrangement of siblings, cousins, aunts and uncles, and—in later years—nieces and nephews, whose names and faces I struggled yearly to connect.

Some, a handful, I saw regularly and was fond of. My Uncle Jack and Aunt Peggy, who would later be my guardians—and salvation—whose home in Connecticut would become mine; and their three sons, who would be like brothers. My father's sister, from Delaware, her husband, and their four, then five, children. My two half brothers, half a generation older than me, on vacations from Yale and St. Paul's.

Others I saw only on Christmas nights, though they greeted me—every one—with kisses and backslaps and fond, informed queries about my progress in life:

My Uncle Lew from Arizona, Granny's nephew, who'd been ambassador to Great Britain under Truman and budget director under Roosevelt, and wore an eye patch from an old fly-fishing accident and told marvelous stories of life in the Southwest. An older cousin—it may have been the same one who married the Rockette—who came to dinner once in knee socks and a kilt of Douglas tartan, and played the bagpipes to the tune of Scottish ballads. My cousin Kitty, tall and blond and white-skinned, whom I secretly coveted, and her husband, Nick, who would be a senator from New Jersey, then treasury secretary under Bush.

All of these were regulars. There were a handful, too, who dropped in and out from year to year, befuddling me constantly with the task of linking first cousins to second, aunts and uncles to brothers and nephews, and myself to everyone there. I never mastered this fully. Even today it is a challenge. But each new confusion added to my wonder. My family, I came to know, was very large, mostly rich, and—in general—kind and gracious and happy with their lives. I wished often that I saw more of them (especially Kitty), and that our lives were more like theirs.

My father always gave the first toast. It was roughly the same from Christmas to Christmas: dewy-eyed and full of high sentiments, a paean to his mother. Granny, who could hear scarcely a word of it from her place at the far end, would lean forward and nod rhythmically, accepting the applause and the "here-heres" with thin smiles and aimless gestures, as though she understood perfectly, which she no doubt did. Then she would settle back in her chair, which would seem to swallow her, and look out at us all from behind the frosted white lenses that hid her cataracts from the world.

The toasts that followed were a mix of the high-minded, the silly, and the mildly off-color: tradition, the bonds of family, the similarities between brook trout and old-maid virgins. The bawdier ones would be delivered in guarded tones, usually by diners at my father's end. Granny would lean forward again with all of her tiny bulk, her neck barely clearing the tabletop, and tip her head to favor her less-deaf ear, then finally give up and lean back with that same little smile, understanding nothing and everything. And the whole table, children and adults, would laugh gaily at her confusion.

It was at Christmas dinner in 1962, when I was eighteen, that my father gave his last toast.

"Have you looked at your father's eyes?" my sister-in-law, sitting to my right at the table, asked me as we sat together watching him toast his mother, awaiting his invitation to raise our glasses. I said I had not.

"They're yellow," she said.

He went into the hospital two days later, with infectious hepatitis, and never came out. He died within a month.

For two more Christmases after that, we went lamely through the motions. My Uncle Jack, in his stead as second son, took my father's place at the head of the table. The Jew jokes were missing and mourned, the Champagne flowed less freely, we were gone before eleven.

Then it was Granny's turn. In the summer of 1965, twenty-nine months after burying her son, she was laid next to him, and to her husband, in the family plot in upstate New York. She was ninety-two. We gathered at her grave as we had gathered, for more than twenty years, at her teas and at her table—to link future with past, to remind ourselves that we were family. Only Granny could have done that for us.

Her apartment was sold after that: Jean and Delia and Hugh and the others put out to pasture on generous annuities, the art and furniture apportioned among us, the will read, the money divided.

I got a card and a wedding-check, eight years later, from Uncle Lew, four months before he died. I ran into the Rockette-cousin at a friend's party and learned that he'd been divorced for years. I saw Kitty once on the street in New York—she looked straight at me, then through me, we both kept walking—and thought her nearly as lovely as ever. I see Nick sometimes on TV, discussing bank failures or the budget, and read his name at least weekly in the paper.

I sold the painting I inherited from Granny, a Maude Earl oil of a blue heron that had hung on the wall in her dining room, several years ago to get out of a jam. I told myself I'd never liked it anyway, and in truth I hadn't. But it had hung dutifully in every home I'd lived in, and when I sold it I felt like I was selling Christmas.

Every family, I think, has had its Granny: the ancient matriarch (or patriarch), the last of her line, who carries the ways and values of the past, undiluted, as far into the future as time and science will permit. She is seen sometimes as dotty and comical, other times only as dear, but when she goes, there is always the certain knowledge, however dim or fleeting, that something irreplaceable has been taken, that a connector no longer connects.

The world that Granny linked us to was a simpler one than ours. It was a world in which, as she had known it, distinctions of class were unchallenged, frontiers awaited the enterprising, and fortunes were earned overnight. The "Good Names" of her day—Astor, Du Pont, Morgan, Mellon, Pulitzer, Rockefeller, Vanderbilt, and others, including her father—were men who traded in deeds of charity and achievement so vast and so visible that they were legends long before they were gone.

Their children, like Granny, were witnesses to these deeds (she was a teenager when her father built his fortune in the 1880s), and to the banks, railroads, factories, newspapers, and foundations they spawned. It was a legacy far more personal, though less lasting, than the millions they would inherit.

With it came, among Granny's class at the turn of the century, a certain easy—though not careless—confidence, a sureness of place and purpose, that was fed by understanding. A sureness worlds apart from the craven, self-asserting poses that would typify so many, like my father, in the generation to follow, removed by time and taxes from the sources of its wealth.

Granny wore her sureness like a second skin. My father told Jew jokes and talked about codes. She was aloof, even austere, around strangers. He was desperate for recognition from headwaiters. She was her father's child. He spent a lifetime inventing himself and never even managed that.

I believe, I have always believed, that the reason I knew nothing as a child of my grandfathers, or of their fathers or mothers or of anyone who'd gone before, was that my father couldn't have risked the comparisons he feared I might draw—that he himself had drawn already, years before.

At Columbia Law School, the dropout son of an alumnus and trustee, who'd spurned his father's dream of a partner's seat in the family firm. The grandson of an empire-builder who could barely meet his sons' tuitions. A failed first marriage, a second that would end in suicide. Thirty years in the brokerage business without distinction. He was ashamed. A failure, he felt, as a man and as a Douglas.

And so he made up stories: of walking five miles to school, through a foot of snow, every winter as a boy; of sweeping the floors of the Stock Exchange to earn his seat; of a near-miss as an Olympic soccer goalie.

Or insulted the seats of his failures: Columbia as "kike heaven," the legal profession as a pack of "goddamn weasels." Or found scapegoats—Roosevelt, the Jews—or melted worthiness into a firm handshake.

He was a bitter, tormented man, haunted by a past he could neither renounce nor live up to. And so he betrayed it, and himself in the process.

He faced this, I believe—briefly, through a whiskey haze—in the last days of his life. I saw his pain and pitied him, though my understanding, at eighteen, was shallow and muddied by anger.

I feel more sympathy today, less pity. More clarity, with less to lose. I wonder sometimes at the man he might have been if his name had been Mahoney. Or if his given name had not been the same as his father's, or his mother had not been quite so rich or lived quite so long.

The dreams he chased then might have been his own. Whatever *they* were, if he even knew. His failures might have been more private. He might not have had to lie.

Six

America is full of James Douglases. . . . They stretch in a long line of rugged, intellectual, capable men, back to the remote Sir James of Castle Dangerous, who knew in his medieval way how to make his name respected. . . .

—The Mining and Scientific Press, June 1918

Granny's father, at the time she was born—in Quebec City, in 1872—was in his middle thirties, and depressed with his life.

"[I was] an obscure redictus," he would write later, "struck by the dreariness of [my] prospects."

It would be nearly half a century before he would recall this, as a bit of self-history codiciled to his will—a will that would leave, in 1918, an estate of more than $20 million, roughly a fifth of which would pass to Granny.*

---

*Granny's father was James Douglas. Her surname, therefore, was the same as her married one—Edith Douglas Douglas—an accident of marriage that broadened my confusion at Christmas parties.

"At middle life," the New York *World* reported in 1918 in its worshipful epitaph to my great-grandfather, "he uprooted himself . . . tore up the sheepskin of family tradition handed on to him by his physician father, and cut into new paths. At 81, he left his heirs a million a year, at the safe ratio of five percent."

It's a tired, heroic image: the black-sheep son beating his own, uncharted path to fortune. Had it been true, the story of James Douglas's millions would be the story of only one life. And the line it traced to Granny and to my father would be shorter and shallower, and in the end less sad.

James's father, also James—grandfather to Granny, great-great-grandfather to me—was a Scot, born in Brechin in the county of Angus in May of 1800. His father, George Douglas, a Methodist minister for more than sixty years, "left a short account of himself," according to his grandson: "a kindly, considerate, hard-working, earnest, simple-minded man."

James, son of George, was indentured at thirteen as medical apprentice to a doctor in Penrith in the county of Cumberland.

"I had to visit the pauper class," he would write in his journals more than half a century later, "as well in the country as in the town. . . . As perquisites, I had the shilling, which was the fee for blood-letting or tooth-drawing. . . . It was the custom of the country people, generally to be bled every Spring."

His apprenticeship lasted five years, ending a month before his eighteenth birthday. James's world then widened overnight. Between the spring of 1818 and the autumn of 1823, he practiced doctoring on four seas and three continents: as ship's surgeon to a whaler on the Greenland Sea; in Calcutta, where he lived with missionaries and treated cholera in the hospital at Dum-Dum; and finally on the Mosquito Coast of Honduras, where he nearly died of yellow fever as doctor to a colony of settlers, half of whom died themselves.

All this left him, he would write later, with "a knowledge of men and things . . . of habits of thought, study and self-reliance."

In June 1823, still half-dead with fever, he was taken off Honduras aboard a British warship and dropped in Belize, sixty miles north, where he was treated by doctors, then "placed in lodging with a very kind negress."

Sometime in September of that year, still too weak to walk or dress himself: "I have a dim idea of a gentleman visiting and praying with me . . . and offering me a passage to Boston, and sometime after, of his heading a procession of sailors who carried me on board of a schooner in a hammock slung on an oar."

So it was that my family came to America.

From Boston, in the early summer of 1824, James sailed for New York, intending to return from there to England. What happened over the weeks that followed could serve as the plot line for a Hardy novel.

In the course of a side trip on the Erie Canal—"because it would be a pity to [leave] without seeing something more of the United States"—James had landed briefly in Utica, New York, and was killing time in Amos Gay's Hotel, when word came that a local farmer had run himself through with the handle of a pitchfork. He was summoned to assist—went to the farmhouse, removed the "plug of clothes" that had been carried by the pitchfork into the farmer's abdomen, and closed the wound. The man recovered without incident.

"I awoke the next morning and found myself famous. Surgical practice poured in on me, and determined me to remain in Utica until the Spring, and then be guided by circumstances.

"Circumstances did guide me. I became attached to a most amiable and talented young lady. . . . I built me a house, I married, I sent to England for my young brother George, and settled down to practise, with the intention of spending my life in Utica."

He remained there two years, built a practice, lectured at the local college, and was "extremely happy in my domestic relations." His departure, in March 1826, was as freakish and sudden as everything else that had befallen him in his adopted land.

It was a common practice among doctors of the day—though illegal, and punishable by prison—to rob graves of the recently dead, dissect and study the cadavers, then return them to the ground. My forebear, it seems, tried this once too often.

"A Scotch lad, without friends, had died at a factory in Hartford, about four miles from town; instead of his body, mistaking the grave, I got that of a well known and highly respected citizen. A few days later, being suddenly called out, I left my office door unlocked. . . . On my return, I found a stage-driver, who finding no one in the office below, had gone upstairs, and was looking at his old employer. . . .

"As soon as he was gone . . . Mrs. Douglas and I packed up a few things, I harnessed my horse to a small sleigh, called a pung, and lost no time in getting into Canada by crossing the St. Lawrence on the ice, at Ogdensburg. . . . I arrived [in Quebec] on a fine afternoon, the 13th March, 1826."

James, not yet twenty-six, had found his home. He would remain in Quebec half a century, raise a family, found a hospital, build and lose a fortune, and leave behind a legacy of humanity and reform that would touch the lives of thousands with its mercies.

"He was a superb man," his son James would write of him nearly a century later. It would be a different world if all of us could say that of our fathers.

He prospered, almost from the start. By early 1832, his surgical practice, especially in the treatment of "club feet and for the cure of squinting," was known throughout the province. Then, in June of that year, as he would recall later in his journals: "The citizens of

Quebec woke up [to find] the Upper town, the Lower town, and the different suburbs, dotted with the bodies of the dead and dying. It would require the pen of DeFoe to describe the awful scenes of death, sin and misery which I witnessed during that awful visitation of the cholera."

The disease would claim thirty-two hundred lives. James, the only doctor in Quebec with experience in treating it—in Calcutta, ten years earlier—saw his practice multiply overnight.

"I was so constantly occupied, that during that season I rarely, if ever, had an undisturbed night's rest."

But there was more to his life than cholera and clubfeet. In the forty-nine years he would pass in Quebec, he would bury one wife and marry a second, father four sons—though only one would outlive him—spend at least nine winters abroad, lecture throughout Canada on the virtues of temperance—and fish, passionately (like almost every other Douglas male in the four generations since), for trout.

"There was only an Indian trail through the woods beyond Lamotte's, and anglers from town rarely went higher than La Prairie. The best pools and rapids had been named by the Indians, Falbosse, Canoe, Grande Roche. . . . The trout were very fine, from half a pound to four, and occasionally to six pounds each."

(His son James, who published his father's memoirs twenty-four years after his death, could not resist a postscript: "One has only to go fifteen miles above Laval to get as good fishing as my father got 70 years ago.")

In winter, with the rivers frozen, he hunted moose: tracking them for days, on snowshoes, with Huron Indian guides pulling toboggans of bacon and biscuits, then shooting and eating them on the spot. "I have eaten venison," he would write, "in all quarters of the globe."

At least one moose, apparently, was spared this fate. A former student, indentured briefly to James in Quebec, reported years later that, at the foot of a circular staircase in his home, "stood a huge stuffed moose, with immense horns . . . and nearly every celebrity of the day who visited Quebec called and asked permission to see the moose . . . Charles Dickens, the Marquis of Waterford, Lord Charles Wellesley . . . but all have gone now to the 'spirit land.' Where the moose is, I do not know."

If there was a theme to my great-great-grandfather's life-work, any single thread that linked all its phases and fragments, it was his obsession with suffering—of almost any sort.

"There lay in his nature," his son wrote of him after his death, "a depth of tenderness, which never came to the surface more attractively than in the presence of pain. . . . His office was a clinic for the poor, long before the word was used in its present sense."

He experimented endlessly with primitive anesthetics: chloroform (it "caused a deterioration of the system," he wrote) and mesmerism, which he used once to cut away half the lower jawbone of a patient who, though he "distinctly heard the sawing across of the bone, [and was] fully aware of my dividing the softer parts . . . said that he felt no pain."

His journals include many such accounts and digressions: on grave-robbing, forensic medicine, patient-doctor relations, medical quackery, homeopathy, the treatment of typhus.

But for all the theories he nourished and the sufferings he eased, nothing else would claim him as totally as the cause he adopted in 1845, and to which he gave himself—abandoning his practice, some of his reputation, and much of his savings—for the next twenty years.

It was the richest contribution of his life and the chief source of his legacy. It is the cause to which Quebec's Douglas Hospital today remains dedicated.

There were three mental asylums in the province in the early 1840s. In all three, which were run on behalf of the province by various orders of nuns, conditions were typical of the day. Inmates were confined to cells roughly eight feet square, and allowed to leave them only once every eight days for as long as it took to mop down the floors.

"Light was admitted through a small window, or bull's eye, in each cell, and the only ventilation was through a grilled opening above the door, by which also heat entered from a corridor. An open trough in each cell, leading into an open drain, carried off the excreta.

"The inmates were debarred intercourse with the world and with each other, were left to brood over their disordered fantasies until they became maniacal, tore their clothes, became filthy in their habits . . . became imbecile or idiotic. . . . One had been confined 28 years, several upward of 20 years. . . . Most of them had never been allowed to leave the cells."

In the spring of 1845, in a contract with the province of Quebec, James and two partners—with him as majority partner—took over from the nuns the care of the inmates at all three asylums. What happened in the years that followed, from all I can tell, was unparalleled on this continent.

They bought a farm at Beauport, four miles north of Quebec City on the St. Lawrence, with a view of both city and river. By the end of 1845, under James's guidance, all of the province's inmates had been collected there.

"They arrived chained and handcuffed. We were informed by their keepers that some of them had been kept fastened to staples driven into the floors of their cells. . . . When approached, they shewed a disposition to bite. . . . One, a man of education and talents, whose mind was in fragments but whose recollection of a confinement of 28 years was most vivid, wandered from window to window. He saw Quebec, and knew it to be a city; he knew ships and boats on the river and bay, but could not comprehend steamers. . . . He remarked that he had been a long time shut up, and that it was 19 years since he had last seen leather. . . ."

From the first day of their treatment at Beauport, James's patients were kept in cells that allowed air and light; they ate communally in dining rooms, were given exercise, sometimes jobs, allowed in many cases to roam the grounds, and seen regularly by doctors. Restraints and seclusion were kept to a minimum, music was played and hobbies encouraged. There were even dances.

"The Thursday evening ball began with the opening of the Asylum," his son would remember later, "and he never failed to attend it himself."

James, whose understanding of mental illness was as primitive as anyone else's in the mid-1800s, had only compassion as his guide: "the conviction that the greatest amount of good was to be effected by an uniform and unvarying system of conciliation and kindness."

"There was never a medical superintendent more beloved by his patients than he was," his son wrote later. "They called him in all sincerity their father. . . . He possessed that rare tact, so essential to all who control the insane, of throwing them off the scent of their false fancies, without contradicting and irritating them."

He was a quarter-century ahead of his peers. South of the border, in Massachusetts, Dorothea Dix was only now, in the mid-1840s, launching her crusade to remove the mentally ill from state prisons. The results of James's humanity, by the standards of his day, were unheard of.

"The effects were soon apparent in their improved health and spirits," he wrote in his report to the province in 1849. "They became stronger, and ate and slept better. Some of them were restored to reason. . . .

"Of all those admitted during the past three years, 43 only have been recent cases. Of these, 21 have been discharged, cured, and only 2 have had a return to mental illness."

With all that, the deck was stacked miserably against progress. The cure rate of patients who had come to Beauport from other asylums, usually after long and brutal confinements, was not nearly as high. Many came from jails; others were incurable or senile, "sent to the Asylum after having exhausted the sympathies of their friends, and worn out even their hope of death. One, an aged man of 82, and paralytic, was brought a distance of 180 miles, to die within two hours."

James's contract with the province allowed an expense of thirty-seven and a half cents per patient per day. It was a ceiling he couldn't—or wouldn't—stay under. By the late 1850s, he was operating the asylum at a loss. By 1865, the drain had grown critical. In the fall of that year, worn out by twenty years of battling with province governors to improve the terms of the agreement, depressed by the endless "calculation of profits from the treatment of the most helpless of all afflicted creatures," James sold his contract at cost.

He was sixty-five and would live ten more years in Quebec before leaving with his son James to live out his life in the United States. By his own reckoning, no doubt, he had failed in his mission with the hospital.

"The idea of an Asylum is still associated with dark cells, with furious madness, chains, straw, filth, and nakedness. Some time will yet elapse ere the friends of insane persons in Canada will send them to an Asylum for the mere purpose of cure, with the full assurance that as much quiet, cleanliness, order and subordination exist, as in any Hospital for the cure of any other disease."

The time would come sooner than he thought. Four years after his death, in 1890, what is today Douglas Hospital opened its doors to a hundred and thirty-nine patients. More than a century later, now serving nearly four thousand, it is among the largest hospitals in Canada.

Its mission—as stated today by James's great-grandson, a member of its board—remains rooted in the principle of its founding: that "the mind, body and spirit are tied together," and that "the best way to treat sickness in any one of them is with love, sympathy, understanding, and above all, with dignity. . . ."

James, son of James—Granny's father—was eight years old when his father opened the asylum at Beauport. He was twenty-eight when its contract was sold. The legacy of those years—of mercy and service, and what he would one day describe as "the qualities of greatness" his father had possessed—wrote itself into every chapter of James's life and work.

He lived eighty-one years, took risks beyond imagining, built cities in the desert and railroads to connect them, put generations of men to work, and gave millions to cure disease. He was, by the time of his death in 1918, one of the richest men in America, and one of its most beloved, eulogized by bankers, statesmen, college presidents, industrialists, and newspapers in twenty states. Nearly all made mention of his fortune; almost none made more than that:

"His voice, his influence and his purse were at the service of every cause that was worthy and every work and plan that had improvement . . . at heart," the Arizona newspaper that knew him best would write after his passing. "He made men happy . . . in the spirit that one comrade helps another."

He had wanted to be a minister. In 1858, at twenty-one, James left Canada for Edinburgh, where he studied three years, passed his examination for the clergy, then—because he couldn't reconcile church doctrine with his own beliefs—declined to sign the Confession of Faith.

He was never ordained, but returned instead to his father's hospital in Quebec. For most of the next four years, the two men managed the asylum together.

"I was studying medicine to qualify myself to be my father's partner and successor," young James wrote later. "I had been brought up among the insane, and was fond of them. . . ."

He never finished his studies. The Beauport contract was sold in 1865, and James was out of work: at twenty-eight, an unordained minister and unlicensed doctor with nothing but character to show for seven years of training. It was not a script for greatness.

But like his father, he was prone to happy accidents. And what happened over the next ten years—for all of what the New York *World* would write in its epitaph half a century later—was more accidental than heroic. James tore up no "sheepskins." And if he "cut into new paths," which you could say that he did, it was only because the old ones had failed to be of use.

His father, it seems, was a better doctor than businessman.

"In his business transactions," James wrote, "my father displayed a strange mixture of distrust and credulity. He refused to invest his savings in the ordinary repositories . . . but he unhesitatingly invested them in enterprises of which he understood absolutely nothing. . . ."

One of these was copper mining. In the late 1840s, a large bed of very rich copper ore had been discovered in Leeds, near Quebec's Megantic River. Other beds had been mined nearby in the years since, though by the early 1860s profits had dried up and the Harvey Hill Mining and Smelting Company was preparing to close up shop. About that time, as James reports it: "My father passed through London on his way to Egypt in the winter of 1863–64. Satisfied that the mine was all that his fancy . . . pictured it as being, and confident, as usual, in his luck and his judgement, he offered the English shareholders to buy all their stock at a ridiculous figure and to pay all their debts."

It's hard to believe it was quite this simple, but the effect was the same. James's father mortgaged most of what he owned to meet the purchase price; the mine flopped badly, he turned over his stake in it to his creditors to meet payments, sold all that was left of his land to pay the mortgages on it, then left for Pennsylvania with his son.

It didn't happen overnight—it would be ten years from purchase to collapse—and young James worked valiantly to prevent it. He applied himself: visiting, then managing, his father's mining properties, widening his small knowledge of geology and mineralogy, learning all he could of the properties and prospects of copper ore.

In the end, his efforts were of no benefit to his father, except to prolong his decline. "His mining operations . . . engulfed his whole estate and left him without property or resource at an age when he could not possibly retrieve his fortunes."

But for the younger James they were an apprenticeship to the building of an empire.

He must have been a brilliant man. A six-month tutelage under a geologist named Hunt gave birth, within less than two years, to what became known as the "Hunt-Douglas method" of refining copper ore. From that point on, one foot followed another. By the early 1870s—the time of Granny's birth—James was doing lecture tours on two continents. In 1875, bankrolled by investors, he left Canada to apply his new process at a mine in Pennsylvania. His father, an old man now, went with him, as he would again six years later, when James moved north from Pennsylvania to New York.

"He had spent half a century in Quebec. . . . He hoped and believed [in his mining investments] as long as he remained there, but when his hopes were finally shattered and his beliefs proved groundless, he gave up his property, and, what was harder still, his reputation for shrewdness, without a murmur. . . . He left all care with his shattered fortune behind him in Canada, and the last years of his life were peaceful and happy."

Young James was thirty-eight when he left Quebec. He had been married fifteen years, since his divinity school days, to the daughter of a British commodore, and was father to five of the six children he would have. Granny, three years old at the time, was his youngest.

The home they moved to in Phoenixville, Pennsylvania, was "an old stone house with a glazed veranda . . . where my father made and painted plaster casts from the squeezes we had taken from the temple walls of Egypt. . . ."

For the time being, James was more respected than rich. But the riches would come. In early 1881, at the request of William E. Dodge of the Phelps Dodge Company, he traveled to Arizona to assess the prospects of a copper claim, the Atlanta Mining tract at Bisbee. He was impressed with the ore he saw, and advised the company to purchase the claim, which it did, for forty thousand dollars.

For his services, James was offered a choice of options: a flat fee or a ten percent interest in the mine. He chose the percentage.

"On that sudden impulse," he wrote years later, "depended my whole subsequent career—successful beyond anything I had ever dreamed. . . ."

By the early summer of 1884, Phelps Dodge had sunk eighty thousand dollars into the property, without results. James persuaded the company to risk a final fifteen thousand. Days later, in mid-July, a large bed of ore was found two hundred feet below the surface. At almost the same time, a second mining firm, the Copper Queen Company, plowed into the same ore bed from the opposite direction. The two companies haggled, then merged into one—the Copper Queen Consolidated Mining Company—of which James became president in 1885.

Over the next twenty-three years, the mines would produce 730 million pounds of copper, yielding more than $30 million to its stockholders in dividends alone. By the time of James's death, the *Wall Street Journal* would note in his obituary, production was exceeding 180 million pounds a year, roughly seven percent of all the refined copper in the world.

The Copper Queen legacy—divided, subdivided, dissipated, or augmented by marriage or investment—remains the bulk of our family's dwindling fortune.

Phelps Dodge meanwhile was building a kingdom on its copper beds. Between 1885 and 1900, throughout Mexico and the Southwest, the company widened its claims, erected mines and smelters and brought in the men to work them, laid railroads, and opened towns.

In 1897, again on the advice of James, the company bought one of its largest claims to date—the Nacozari mines in Sonora, Mexico—and three years later built its largest smelter, midway between Nacozari and the Copper Queen, to refine the ore from both properties.

A town took shape around that smelter, flush on the border between Arizona and Mexico, forty miles southeast of Tombstone. It was James who planned the town, and it was for him that it was named.

Twenty years later, the week following his death, the Douglas, Arizona, *Dispatch* would write of its patron:

There are two kinds of developers of a country's resources—those who blaze a pathway to achievement for profit only, and those who have a passion for success but do not crave it unless it brings with it a measure of good for those whose toil is to a great extent responsible. Douglas belonged to the latter. . . . [In planning Douglas] He wanted a beautiful city of contented people, a city of homes owned by those who lived in them, independent, managing its own affairs, progressive, alert, loyal. . . .

To link its smelter to markets in the East, Phelps Dodge built a railroad from Douglas to El Paso—the El Paso Southwestern—which replaced the twenty-mule teams that had been hauling ore up to a hundred miles each way. James planned the railroad, oversaw its completion, and was named its president. Several years after that, in 1909, he became president of Phelps Dodge itself.

Southern Arizona was no longer a frontier. But its progress had never been steady. It was a lawless, greedy time in the Southwest—the time of Wyatt Earp and Doc Holliday, Cochise and Geronimo, silver strikes and cattle wars. There were mine fires at the Copper Queen, Apache raids against railroad workers. By 1906, three new companies had arrived to compete, and the thousands of immigrants who flowed in after them brought organized labor, mine strikes, blacklists, scabs, and violence.

The Copper Queen struggled and bent badly, but never broke. By the start of World War I, it was the largest source of copper in the nation. James, an old man by then, served two more years as president of Phelps Dodge, was succeeded by his son Walter, and took his last position as chairman of its board.

Two years after that, in 1918, only months before his death, he retired. He had served the company thirty-seven years—as engineer, planner, settler, and industrialist—and had written his name into the history of the Southwest. More than that, he had made it loved.

"He was both a great and a good man," wrote the Bisbee, Arizona, *Review* in mourning his passing. "He loved the Southwest, where he had wrestled mightily with great problems, and done great things. . . . His imprint is upon the [land], graven as deep as the deepest shaft in any mountainside . . . deeper still in the hearts of the hundreds of men who were here in the old days and knew Douglas, face to face and man to man. . . . When they speak of him, it is not of the scientist, the writer, the organizer that they speak. It is of the man."

He had been a millionaire at least twenty years when he retired, and had earned millions more than he would keep. His philanthropies were legion. Having lost a daughter to cancer in 1910, he gave six hundred thousand dollars to establish New York Memorial Hospital (today Sloan-Kettering) as a national center for cancer research. In 1914, he became the first of seven Douglases to sit on its board, and the first of three to head it. He backed the war effort with $1 million in war bonds, endowed universities in Arizona and Quebec, hospitals in Quebec and Ontario, and the Museum of Natural History in New York.

Five of his six children would outlive him. One of them was Granny. Another was his oldest son, James—third in the line—a gritty, hard-living cowboy-miner, a millionaire in his own right till he gave most of it away. They knew him in Arizona as Rawhide Jimmy; he wore work clothes with red suspenders and smashed chairs in board rooms. His best friend was Georges Clemenceau.

Rawhide died when I was four; I never knew him. I knew his son, though: Uncle Lew, the eye-patched ambassador who told stories at Granny's parties. A gentle, kind-smiling man, he was a close friend to Churchill and Eisenhower; his "personal hero" was a teenage railroad engineer named Jesus Garcia, who'd steered a burning mine train away from a Mexican village, to his death, in 1907.

But the "greatest man" Lewis ever knew, he wrote in his journal several years before his death, was his grandfather James.

During the last decade of his life, needing perhaps to close the circle on his roots, James returned once a year to his father's hospital in Beauport, which by then had reverted to the custody of nuns. Of the eight hundred patients he had left there, he would write following his first trip back, only two remained. One of these, "dear old Ellen Cleary, after a parting of nearly twenty years, fell upon my neck and kissed me. The lady superior must have been touched, but the rules of her order evidently obliged her to turn her back."

James died on June 25, 1918, at his home in Spuyten Duyvil, New York, overlooking the same stretch of the Hudson from which his father, nearly a century before, a twenty-three-year-old itinerant still weak with typhus, had sailed upriver to a future he had not foreseen.

My father was fourteen when his grandfather died. They fished together, several times, in the Adirondacks.

I like to imagine what they would have talked about, the empire-builder and his grandson, huddled together in a lean-to waiting out a rainstorm. Scotland perhaps, or Arizona cowboys, or the six-pound trout in the Prairie River pools James had fished with his father as a boy.

I wonder what my father thought of the old man. Probably nothing—just that he was an old man, too timid and feeble to get across the rocks to the pools on the far side of the river where the big trout lay.

Seven

Aristocrat. It's a disused term today, a dinosaur-word with faintly malevolent connotations: bigotry, elitism, cobwebbed patrimonies, old men in oak rooms nodding off over stock quotes.

It has been corrupted, largely, by irrelevance—by generations of trust-funded Toms and Daisys who mistake arrogance for character and class for a cocoon. They are cartoon figures, most of them, who do credit to the parodies they evoke. For the most part, though, they are harmless.

Then there are the frightened ones—the dangerous ones—the ones for whom rank and privilege are not a birthright but a scepter. Blind, misguided men and women for whom decadence and bigotry become a code of life, who betray their early dreams, defraud those foolish enough to believe in them, then turn against the world for its failure to keep a promise.

I read the journals and letters of my ancestors today—especially of my father's father—and it's not hard to see where young "Billy" Douglas got the promptings that would color his world. It was a different time then. Old money was still almost new, class was more than perception, aristocrats were *real*. The message they set their world by was the message he perverted: that privilege carries with it the responsibility of fair play, that the moral standard for society should be set by its best-educated—and thereby enlightened—members. That any blessings that come of this privilege should be shared for the greater good.

It is an ethic that relies more or less equally on the virtues of honor, sacrifice, responsibility, and good sense. In its purest version, its original version, it is a formula for enlightened nobility—noblesse oblige—as basic and inarguable as helping an old lady across the street.

There are those, still, who practice it. My father's younger brother, as decent a man as I've ever known, gave back to the world ten times what he ever took from it. But there are at least as many who don't. Because it is an invitation to self-congratulation, to the moral deceit that hides behind rank and ignores responsibility.

For men such as these, frightened, backward-looking men weighted down by expectation, aristocracy is like a raft in a tide pool. You drift on it, it holds you afloat, till the tide comes in again and you are borne out to sea without a paddle.

My father's father, Archibald Douglas, an aristocrat if ever there was one, died three weeks before his oldest son's fortieth birthday. It was December 1943, six months before D-Day; I was a small swelling on my mother's belly, and would never hear his name mentioned. Granny, seventy-one at the time, would be a widow twenty-one years.

It is hard to know, from the perspective of my father's life, if his father died too soon or lived too long. He set a shining standard for his namesake and eldest son, loved him unconditionally—sometimes blindly—dreamed dreams for him that would never be realized, and died, no doubt, disappointed. He would never admit this, even to himself. But my father, I'm sure, knew it well.

His life would be a benchmark for any son. There were no empires carved in the line that led to him, no fortunes on the scale of the Copper Queen that would sustain four generations of nannies, trust funds, summer camps, and private schools. The privilege of his line had been earned more patiently, less conspicuously—law, the ministry, journalism, business. And there is a humility that runs through it, a deference to God, women, and fellow man, that is somehow lacking in the line of Jameses.

He was born in 1872 in Tarrytown, New York, the second of three children. His father, Henry Douglas, an invalid the last twenty-five years of his life, is never mentioned in his journals. The text of a minister's eulogy, pasted in a scrapbook, remembers him as "a born gentleman, cultured by education and social intercourse, in the rectitude and moral grandeur of his principles. . . ."

The real moral force in my grandfather's early life was an uncle, John Waldo Douglas, a Presbyterian minister and missionary to California in the early days of the gold rush. His Uncle John, who had never married, became like a father to his brother's oldest boy—until one morning, on a hunting trip together in the north woods of the Adirondacks in the early 1880s, when his young nephew couldn't wake him.

"His force of character and fine and fashioned Christianity so impressed me," my grandfather would remember nearly thirty years later—two years after he had christened his second son, John Waldo Douglas, my father's younger brother, as his uncle's namesake.

My grandfather was a lawyer with a poet's soul. As a student at Columbia in the mid-1890s, he studied literature and wrote verses for whomever would publish them, was briefly editor of a poetry magazine, then of the *Columbia Literary Monthly,* before graduating from the law school in 1896 as president of his class.

It was Granny, he wrote later, who cured him of his "sentimental nonsense." They had met in 1890, at her father's home in New York. They would not marry until eleven years later, but her influence was immense.

"Edith turned me to thinking in a worthy way," he wrote in his journal in 1919, by then founder-partner of a New York law firm. "I would have drifted on indefinitely, might never have reached anywhere. . . . There is not much time for poetry [anymore]. One must have matured some at 47."

They had, by his telling, a remarkable marriage. She read him to sleep at night, he sent her violets every Easter for forty-three years, and wrote that "a very great blessing had been preserved for me in the great chance of life."

Nine years before his death, on a trip to Atlantic City in the spring of 1934, he sat by his hotel window one morning at dawn, looked out at the "still and vast sunrise over the Atlantic," and saw in it the constancy of their love.

"Nothing changes fundamentally. . . . We go on together, Edith and I, closer and older and sad sometimes, but what a life to be thankful for. . . ."

For all of his poetic sentiments, my grandfather was an inveterate snob. The current term would be "elitist," and this probably fits more aptly. But these are modern judgments against a turn-of-the-century man. By the standards of the day, he was a "gentleman of his class."

He believed, as gentlemen did then—as his father and father-in-law, James Douglas, had believed before him—in the principle of a "natural aristocracy." The poor and uneducated—the "uncultivated"—were the lower rungs in a social ladder that depended as much on the bottom as on the top. But there could be no blurring of the two.

And by the early 1930s, with taxes now a fixture of life and the Depression at its most punishing, the blurring had begun. It saddened him deeply, and would occupy his thoughts for much of the balance of his life.

In August 1932, following a visit to his boyhood home in Trenton, New York, my grandfather sounded the first notes of a dirge his eldest son—more hollowly, but with far more dissonance—would spend a lifetime vulgarizing:

"It is almost all gone. . . . The charming village, where 100 years ago an intellectual center flourished, has lost its appeal and is reverting to type. The old families have left, and none of worth take their place. The aristocracy lies in the graveyards. . . .

"The beauty of the old streets with the great elms, the delightful peace, has all but vanished. Only the cemetery still keeps its beauty and its names. Do *we* change or does the world?"

His public life was dazzling. It must have cowed my father. By 1903, at the age of thirty-one, my grandfather was a law partner. Seven years later he had his own practice—Douglas, Armitage, in New York—where he would remain the balance of his life. His specialities were mining and real-estate law. From what I can determine, he was unexcelled in either field. His income, which began at $240 a year as a law clerk just out of school, had risen to $10,000 by 1909 and to $40,000 eight years later.

He argued before the Supreme Court, was counsel to a dozen corporations, and sat on the boards of too many companies to name. His closest friend, other than his law partner, was Harlan Stone, chief justice of the Supreme Court. He was a trustee of Columbia, a director of Hahnemann Hospital, and chairman of the board—like his father-in-law before him—of today's Sloan-Kettering.

"I have been successful in law," he wrote in 1919, seemingly awed by the prospect of his own prosperity. "Very successful. Success at a ratio of increase I fear I cannot keep pace with."

His pace was broken, at least briefly, ten years later. The Depression left him, he wrote in 1932, "where I started 35 years ago, my savings gone and my investments almost valueless. So too with Edith. . . . The curve of our prosperity points down. . . . But fortune has been kind to me."

Fortune remained kind. Granny's millions, though depleted, were enough to see them through. They divided their lives, during most of those years, between an apartment on Park Avenue—"an Italian villa, snatched from the Adriatic and dropped into Manhattan"—and the family estate in the Bronx, on a promontory overlooking the Hudson.

I remember the house, though only vaguely: a mansion of gray stone that rambled on forever, ivy-covered and fronted by a circular driveway, with a swimming pool and tennis court in back. No one alive today can remember how many rooms, only that there were too many to use.

My Aunt Peggy, widow of my father's brother Jack, lived there briefly in the early forties: "It was a beautiful house, so gracious and elegant. It went on and on. The stone, I think, had been imported. And the living room—what a room that was—was really a ballroom. Enormous, we never used it. Your uncle and I had some happy times there, some wonderful memories."

My grandfather loved that house. It brought out the poet in him. He would sit at his bedroom window, sometimes for hours, writing of the wonders of what he saw: the "deep purplings of the palisades" on the far shore, "the Hudson silvered with the afternoon sun," "the oak and tulip trees that burst out lush and tender green, then morning by morning grow slowly less delicate."

In 1929, inspired by the birth of his first grandson, he tried for a moment to make of his home an anchor in time:

"In this restless world of ours, the nation pushes on and we become ever more impermanent. . . . I do hope this home of ours, on the river whereon I was born, will become the center for long generations to come, that the young boy will one day bring his family here, and carry on in this spot that we love so keenly. Perhaps we can anchor something, for a time at any rate."

It never happened. The house was sold within ten years of his death, and the riverfront land below it, which he gave to the city for use as a park, is today a fenced-off rectangle, two hundred feet or so from end to end, of weeds, broken bottles, fast-food wrappers, and spent condoms. A small sign, ancient and barely legible—SPUYTEN DUYVIL PARK—marks the entrance, which is padlocked.

He and Granny raised three children in that house. My father, Archibald Douglas Jr.—nicknamed "Billy"—born in the third year of their marriage in January 1904, was the oldest, followed at three-year intervals by a second son and a daughter. A slight, serious boy with a quick mind, a natural brashness, and an early flair for baseball, Billy was an easy fit for his role as firstborn and favorite—a role that, for nearly sixty years after, he had barely to wink to defend.

I suspect he was a happy child. If he wasn't, he couldn't have known it. The first son of privileged parents who took to heart the responsibilities of their rank, he learned books from his mother, trout fishing from his father, and politics at family dinners. He was taught tennis and golf, and took easily to both; he went to Giants games at the old Polo Grounds and attended Broadway openings as a guest of his mother's charities. There were wilderness trips to the Adirondacks, salmon-fishing vacations in Canada, and weekends at the family farm upstate.

By the time he was a teenager, he knew every corner of his father's law office at 280 Broadway—and knew, too, just as surely, that his destiny lay in its shingle. He was *finished* as much as raised, but it must have been wonderful fun.

Still, it wasn't all things and places. My father was spoiled, to be sure, but his parents were far too wise to leave it at that, to trust that a gentleman would bloom from coddlings alone. There were values, too, passed down in that house, by example as well as training:

A rock-strong marriage with respect from both ends, free exchanges of views and interests, rules laid down and lived by, Christmas dinners with seatings for twenty. Time spent, attention paid, traditions rooted. A healthy home, from everything I know of it.

"No one can value the great asset to these [children of ours]," my grandfather wrote the month following my father's eighteenth birthday, "of these days at home as they grow along. . . . Edith a great mother, a wonderful woman, confident of all the family."

My grandfather was the family's voice of wit and reason, the storyteller and gentle guide who dispensed wisdoms, bounced babies, and patched sore egos. But Granny was the anchor—stiff and aloof, even then, with a sense of place and aplomb so soldierly it must have seemed sometimes to obscure her good intentions.

"She was the gendarme," my uncle's widow recalls today. "In the British tradition, the old school. I remember, when I first was seeing your uncle, the year before we were married, and he would invite me to the house, I would always kiss her when we got there—it seemed the natural thing to do. But I could tell she didn't like it, she seemed almost offended, so after a while I just stopped. It was never that way with your grandfather, though. The dearest, warmest man you'd ever want to know."

My father, I think, found himself trapped between styles. A natural chameleon, pulled between the poles of his father's graciousness and his mother's regal airs, he adopted over time the trappings of both, but could manage the essence of neither.

He became a hybrid: the idealist/snob, the bigot/romantic, who would join the Missionary Society at prep school and spend a lifetime defending—against all evidence—his passion for the "little guy," but would draw his "good name" around him like a wall against the world, and slander "kikes" and "niggers" with every breath.

He was never much of a student. There was never much of a need. A private-school education, for the pre-Depression son of a New York law partner wedded to an heiress, rewarded merit as it rewarded home runs, as something to be hoped for—perhaps aimed for—but seldom demanded.

The purpose was to polish, not winnow: a birthrighted, unbroken glide between interconnected sandboxes—grade school, prep school, Ivy League—with progress charted more by the smoothness of the flow than by anything reflected in letters or numbers. Poise acquired, contacts developed (then nurtured, in Yale societies and Princeton eating clubs), a social conscience gardened sparingly. Such were the rudiments of the "Christian schools for young men" before the 1930s and '40s, when "complications of class"—Jews and Irishmen finding their ways to the seats of power—forced them to reassess.

The Riverdale Country School in the north Bronx, today a patchwork of old brick and new concrete spread over two campuses on either side of the Henry Hudson Parkway, nine hundred students strong with an alumni roll that includes Jack Kennedy and Carly Simon, was just three years old when Billy Douglas entered as a first-grader in the fall of 1910. A tiny, boys-only enclave of "humanistic education" (it would not go coed until the 1930s) that served fewer than eighty students from a single wood-frame schoolhouse that still survives, it provided just the sort of early grounding my grandparents had in mind: moneyed schoolmates, jackets and ties required, a healthy smattering of classics and the Bible—chapel was the first order of every day—an all-male faculty that administered discipline with a firm but even hand.

My father passed eight years at Riverdale. With the exception of his prowess at second base, noted frequently in the issues of the *Riverdale Review* that survive him, they were utterly, almost studiously, undistinguished: B's in English, D's in Latin (or in Science, rarely in both), other grades clustered unvaryingly between. It was the beginning of his mastery of the art—he would call it the "science"—of the "Gentleman's C."

This was a principle my father took seriously. He would try vainly, some forty years later, to impart it to me, I suppose after it had become clear to him that my own academic path held as little promise as his had.

I never mastered it, though. By the time he issued his challenge, the D's and F's were exploding like measles over my report cards. So instead, I just flunked out and began again somewhere down the ladder, then repeated the process.

My father was the first of two Douglases at Riverdale, as he would be for eight years after at St. Paul's and Yale. His younger brother Jack, who trailed him by three years through all three schools, marched to a beat my father never even heard. For Jack, in school as in life, there was nothing gentlemanly about C's; they were affirmations of mediocrity, only that. A B showed competence, an A was always the goal.

"Jack's desk was next to mine," Ernest McAneny remembers. McAneny, now in his mid-eighties, was a Riverdale classmate of my uncle's, later a teacher at the school for more than forty years. He is today the archivist for its alumni office.

"I never knew your father—he left the year I came—but Jack was remarkable. A serious boy, a serious student. He'd be always buried in his books, never looking up. He wanted to be the best. I did admire him so much, we all did. You just knew about Jack, whatever he set his mind to, he'd make a go of it. I never saw him again, though, after he left here. Whatever became of Jack, can you tell me?"

I told him: that my uncle had graduated from Yale, married a warm, wonderful woman, fathered three sons, founded a foil mill in Connecticut and guided its growth through thirty years; that he'd been my guardian after my father's death, and that his patience and wisdom—so like his own father's—had been the difference for me. And finally, that he'd died, of cancer, in the spring of 1978.

"Ahhh," said his old classmate. "Then we were right. . . . There was something about Jack, you just knew the world would go well for him."

The world went as well for Jack as it went sadly for my father. It's an old story, really: the coddled first son wasting his early promise on liquor and women, the overlooked younger brother plodding his way earnestly to the top. The Prodigal Son, the Hare and the Tortoise. And with Billy and Jack, from the older one's first breath to the younger's dying day, the script ran true to form.

It began with natural blessings. My uncle was a better-than-average athlete, especially in hockey and baseball, but my father was better still: clean-up hitter, downhill skier, goalie and star of the Yale soccer team. Jack was nice-looking; my father's looks were a ticket through life. ("That smile, the twinkle in those eyes—he could convince you of anything," my uncle's widow says today of her brother-in-law.) Jack had poise; Billy played a crowd like a magician knotting handkerchiefs.

Only in trout fishing—the patient sport, refined over years, with slow artistry as its own reward—was my uncle the better man. My father was a skilled fisherman and loved the sport, but Jack could fish circles around him, and both brothers knew it.

My uncle was never neglected. You couldn't call it that. His parents appreciated his earnestness, ministered to his needs, and—no doubt—parceled their affections in ways they saw as fair. But Billy, hands-down, was the favorite. His closest competition, from all I can gather, came from his younger sister, referred to alternately as "Angel" and "Baby" (foretelling my own sister as "Princess"), and praised often for her charm, poise, and "earnest, easy ways."

Of the more than two hundred and fifty pages in my grandfather's journal—written over forty-seven years, ending a month before his death—nearly half include some praise of Billy: his soccer, his fishing, his "fearlessness," his "keen mind," his "pep and go."

Of Jack, who would be twenty times the man his brother would be, less than half as much is written, but the sense of it is clear: He is "more conventional, more reasoned, studious and steady, a quaint boy and a great angler."

All his life my uncle labored in his brother's shadow, which grew less daunting over the years but never lost its pall. Even in death.

In the fall of 1972, nine years after my father had died and I'd moved into my uncle's house and custody—"our fourth son," my Aunt Peggy called me from the day I got there, despite the miseries I would cause them both—I was a guest at his sixty-fifth birthday. The dining room was full of celebrants, both family and friends. There were toasts from all quarters.

One of the last—perhaps the very last, for it would have been hard to follow—came from a lifelong friend and fishing chum, who'd known both brothers since their days together at Yale. His remembrances, sometimes witty, mostly sodden, frequently off-color, went on and on, as such things often do: drunken sophomore nights, forgotten Vassar girls, the crash of a bush-plane on a fishing outing.

Then, abruptly and with no particular context, the toaster wound up:

"To Jack—fisherman, friend, gentleman, and the finest little brother Archie Douglas could have had."

My uncle must have been wounded—I was wounded for him—but he only smiled and nodded when the glasses were raised around him. He would never have done otherwise.

And if my Uncle Jack were alive today, and knew the direction I was taking with my father's story, he'd advise me to find another book to write. Failing that, he'd cull his mind for every fond memory, every noble word or deed, that he could credit, however loosely, to his older brother. I'm certain that's what he'd do. He was like that. Loyal, fair-minded, forgiving—his father's son.

It's a pity my grandfather never saw it. A kindred spirit, right under his nose. It might have cushioned some of the sadness his oldest son caused him. Life might have gone a little easier for them all.

Eight

$In \mathcal{S}eptember$ 1918, less than two months before the Armistice was signed in France, Billy Douglas entered St. Paul's School. He was our progenitor there, the first of three generations of Douglases (with the fourth now waiting its turn) who would attend the school over the next seven decades: a brother, all three sons, and half of his ten grandchildren.

The slow unfolding of this petty dynasty would become for him, over time, a core credential of his vaunted "good name." A St. Paul's education, he would say to me when I was expelled from it forty-odd years later, is a "testing ground for gentlemen." I had failed, by his accounts, at the highest of all ministries. I had broken the line. I was a "stigma" on our name.

I can't be the only one, over the last half-century, to have suffered these same slurs from a disgraced St. Paul's alumnus. The school, in Concord, New Hampshire, is an institution that cultivates dynasties. There are dozens on its rolls, a few now nearing their fifth generation.

As a center of learning, St. Paul's has meshed well with the times. It is coeducational today, as most such schools are; there is less structure, greater independence, a growing allowance for minorities. But as a name and as a symbol, it remains what it was the day my father entered: the premier destination for the moneyed Eastern schoolboy, rooted in the values of an enlightened aristocracy that may or may not exist, drenched in tradition, nestled in the bosom of the Episcopal Church (headmasters are "rectors"; chapel, for decades, was a daily affair), and driven by implicit assumptions of excellence that stretch from the dorm and classroom to the hockey rink and spring dance.

Billy was fourteen when he entered St. Paul's, and most of what he would become. Handsome, athletic, jaunty, quick-smiling, but with a broodiness that seemed never far below the surface. For most of his first two years, he stayed true to his Riverdale stride—thirty-seventh in a class of sixty-eight, third base on the JV team, several friendships that would carry to Yale and beyond.

Then, in his junior year, for reasons beyond fathoming, he gave out like an old car, finishing with a June exam grade average of 49.8, second to last in his class.

At today's St. Paul's, that would have been the end of the road. It would take far less than that, forty years later, to end *my* career there. But those were different times. The family was alerted. A series of letters, since purged from my father's file at the school ("to protect privacy," the alumni office told me; "we live in litigious times"), passed between rector and father. A meeting was arranged, conditions were set—Billy was invited to return.

Sometime during that summer between his junior and senior years, father and son went fishing together in Canada. The record of that trip, of what passed between them and what sense my grandfather came away with, is preserved in an entry in his journal, dated the following February, 1922:

"Billy had a thorny road for a time at St. Paul's, due to misconstruction and misunderstanding by teachers and boys. We went together to Newfoundland to talk it all over after our days on the Salmon River . . . had some delightful hours there, Billy and I in the little tent together, talking all these questions out. . . . Billy is a delightful, frank, fearless, generous, honest able boy who will hue his own independent way along. . . . By and by, he will learn to take the open path that lies before him, when it is straight and falls to hand. . . . [Meanwhile] he is finishing up creditably."

My grandfather loved well, but not always wisely. It may have been his only great weakness. But for Billy, it was a damning one. There were probably other things in my father's early life that taught him the value of forgery, but his father's blindness was almost certainly the first. He learned to read it perfectly, and to play it like a trout. Any boy would have, given the chance. He learned to lie and smile—maybe even, as early as the Salmon River, to make his eyes mist up on cue. He became a con. And the more it worked—and it always worked, every time, right to the end—the easier it must have gotten. Until it was most of what he knew.

There's no way of knowing what role Granny played in all this, but she had to have been a part. She was a tough old lady by the time I knew her, and even then she saved her softest moments for her son. (He was the only one who could make her forget herself: She would giggle on the couch like a kid, at ninety years old, at any joke he told. The rest of us did well to raise a smile.)

Perhaps she knew the truth all along—she was never the dreamer her husband was—and kept it to herself to save on wear and tear. Or maybe he had them both fooled.

Whoever was fooled or wasn't, Billy's "creditable finish" at St. Paul's was a senior-year final-exam average of 56.5, with a failure in geometry: fifty-seventh in a class of sixty-eight. Even in those benign times, that shouldn't have been good enough for Yale. Somehow it was.

February 1923, two entries later in his father's journal:

"Billy entered Yale in the class of 1926. He was captain of his freshman soccer team, got his class letter and captain's sweater. So far is doing well at his studies, excepting Physics, a stumbling block. He seems to be a leader, and is gaining in poise and perspective, always had confidence. He was 19 last week."

He had found his mountaintop. My father would live forty more years, almost to the day. There would be successes of a sort—financial, political, romantic—and some times he would remember later as happy ones. But there would never be another Yale.

Through three marriages, two careers, and more fresh starts than anyone should be entitled to, he would tell Yale stories, sing Yale songs, drink and fish and commiserate with Yale classmates. It was his totem, his gum and comic book, the Rosebud he would spend a lifetime reliving.

I knew, probably as early as I knew anything about my future, that I was bound for Yale. By way of St. Paul's, to be sure ("the testing ground"). But Yale was the Everest, the final crucible. It would forge me, then knight me, as it had my father. The Gentleman Arrived.

In the spring of 1962, when word came from New Haven that this was not to be, that I would not be among its class of '66—a foregone decision, by that time—my father offered me a choice: Army, Navy, Air Force, or Marines. There would be no talk of other schools, he said, although I had been admitted to two. Yale was "the only college for a son of mine." I enlisted in the Air Force on my eighteenth birthday and lasted ten weeks.

It wasn't that he'd been a success there (as at St. Paul's, he barely made it through). Or even, necessarily, that those were blissful years. They were his "Yale years." If you'd gone to Yale, you understood that; if you hadn't, it was scarcely worth explaining.

He wrote for the freshman yearbook, played baseball and hockey for his class, and goalied the Yale soccer team through three seasons of "erratic brilliancy." He was a member of Zeta Psi and of another, more secret union, the "Gentlemen of the Old School," so arcane (or preposterous, or short-lived) that a search through Yale archives turned up only a single cryptic mention of it, in my father's senior yearbook, notes of the class of '26: "It met quietly and unrestrainedly at Mory's. Archie Douglas invariably opened the old debate, namely, 'was Tom Sweeney truly a gentleman of the Old School or merely a genius of the new?' "

Even at Yale, the self-appointed arbiter of irrelevant standards. The snob in search of a cause.

I don't know when he found time to study, if he ever did. There was apparently a nightly poker game in the room of a classmate named Leeky Wilson, who rarely attended himself. The yearbook explains: "Everyday the janitor shovels out the ashes, which fall sometimes sixteen inches in an evening. Leeky studies downstairs in Archie Douglas' room, and Archie does his best work in Leeky's."

It was, if nothing else, a social four years. There were some rich pickings among the class of '26 at Yale, among the best my father would ever know:

Jock Whitney, the philanthropist-millionaire, who would go on to head the Whitney Foundation and serve as chairman of the Museum of Modern Art. Lucius Beebe, the flinty, eccentric *Herald Trib* columnist, author, and Old West historian, whose cheeky self-update to the *Yale Alumni News* in his twenty-fifth reunion year must have turned my father green with envy: "I have made more money . . . become acquainted with more of the great of the world, and had more of what passes in bed for love than most." Gifford Ewing, a close friend and former St. Paul's classmate, who had shown promise as a poet in his school days but turned instead to oceanography in California. Charley Willard, who would be a professor at the Yale Law School and godfather to my father's first child. Dan Lindley, captain of the Yale baseball team, future brother-in-law and friend for life.

There were many such friends. He had no problem making friends, only sometimes in keeping them. He had flair and warmth, passion and originality, and a wonderful, electric wit that could turn soft or cruel depending on the crowd. And he rarely misread a crowd. He was an entertainer; it was his highest art. He wanted desperately to be liked, and usually was.

He muddled through. I don't know how close he came to not making it—Yale doesn't open its files, even to family, for seventy-five years after graduation—but it must have been close. It would take an end run from his father at the eleventh hour to pull him out:

"Billy may not graduate till fall," my grandfather recorded in his journal in June of 1926, "due to failure to obtain quality rank. I see Dean Jones tomorrow."

So far he had ducked every bullet, and was a Yale man to boot. But the unraveling had begun already. That same month, June 1926, Billy embarked on the road to his first major undisputed failure: a marriage that would end in desertion ten years and two children later.

She was a Barnard girl, a June graduate, with an old New England name, a dimpled, open face to go with her reddish curls, and an energy to match his own. They had known each other more than a year, and announced their intentions in June.

"[Claire] is fine, sweet, jolly and delightful," my grandfather wrote in recording their engagement. "A charming young aristocrat. Her father an able physician in the first flight. . . . This alliance between our families will be satisfactory and long."

They planned to marry the following June. Billy, meanwhile, his Yale diploma now in hand, took his first step on the path to his noblest birthright: the adding of "Jr." to the name on the frosted glass of the partners' office at 280 Broadway. It was a destiny he had been shepherded for since his opening days at Riverdale.

In the fall of 1926, he was enrolled at Columbia Law School. His father, now fifty-four, was ten years from retirement. The timing was ideal.

"Billy will make a successful lawyer," my grandfather predicted, "with more of a love of work still to be developed. This will come in time, with the passing of the theoretical into the practical."

Almost from the start, there were signs of trouble. And signs too—the first yet—of the slow eroding of his father's faith and patience: "[Claire] and Billy to marry June 29 [1927]. Not certain yet if this is best, only time will tell. Yet if B. postpones his wedding till his law [review] and an adequate return, he may wait till doomsday. . . . Not certain yet whether his competitive stand is high enough to pass him on to second year law."

He made it to his second year, and through it, but that was as far as he got. I'm not sure just how the end came. Officially, he dropped out in favor of a brokerage job. What really happened, there's no way of telling, but it almost doesn't matter. He had spurned a birthright.

His father, of course, would forgive him. But the hurt weighed heavily. It would be the only time, in his dozens of journal entries devoted to Billy over nearly forty years, that my grandfather could not conceal his regret. Even then, he tried:

"Billy has concluded to give up law and turn to Wall Street. . . . And he will, I am certain, make good. Still, it would have added much to have been able to pass on the nucleus of this splendid practice we have built up to Billy, to have shared in his professional work. However, all works out well. . . ."

Probably, like other young men of his class and time, my father felt too heavily the weight of others' hopes. He was still young and full of vision, the world was not his father's—at least not *only* his father's—he would find his way in it. And no doubt he tried.

But when he failed, as young men do, when he fell on his face the first time and the second, and looked up from his place on the ground to see what might be left for him, he saw not ahead but behind, not what could still be but what had been wasted and lost forever. The road not taken.

And as he grew older and tireder, and the choices narrowed and the consolations lost their light, his anger turned brittle inside him, then outward against the world. He grew unloving, finally cruel, when all he ever really was was scared.

There was one thing—the only one I know of—that my father adopted, undiluted, from his father. The politics of the Republican moneyed class. For the older man they were an extension of rights and property; their place in his life depended on the threats he perceived. For the younger one, they began as a medium, grew quickly to a cause, and ended as an obsession.

My grandfather was a vintage Hoover Republican: quiet government, unfettered markets, an easy acceptance of the divisions of wealth and class. He had been wounded, though not mortally, by the Great Depression. He believed, as Hoover did, that the economy (which is to say, his prospects) would rebound spontaneously if only left alone. Franklin Roosevelt, with his view of banking regulators, inheritance taxes, and public funds for the disadvantaged, was a threat to the natural balance.

My grandfather was a sometimes misguided, hopelessly uppish, but always benevolent man. He believed the best of people. Even of Stalin, ten years later: "For the misled Stalins one can have pity." And of scores of lesser rogues, crooks, jesters, and philanderers—including his eldest son—who peopled his journal over forty-seven years.

Only twice was he truly unkind. Once was to Hitler: "He and his tyrants are doomed. May the Bible's torments in Hell be understated for them." The other time to FDR: "Franklin Roosevelt, the man, the president, the perhaps potential dictator, the danger. . . . Is the tide turning against him? We hope so. He is a damned curse, a dishonest, self-seeking charlatan."

It was a common theme among families of rank in the early and mid-thirties, that Roosevelt, a fellow blue blood, was somehow a "traitor to his class," that he had broken the trust, violated the code of the sandbox by proposing levies on its wealth (which were never enacted) and watchdogs on the banks and markets whose free-fall had triggered the misery.

It was a cynical notion, and would be forgotten in time. But my grandfather believed it, my father swallowed it whole, and I would grow up—twenty years later—in the knowledge that Franklin Roosevelt was the root cause behind every war, famine, unpaid bill, and thankless nigger that ever threatened the common good. The universal scapegoat. His name was an obscenity in our home.

For now, though, he was a platform, a purpose in life.

"A tense political week," my grandfather reported a month before the '32 election. "The Roosevelt ticket seems strong, but all the family are fighting hard for Hoover. Billy speaking every night."

He spoke well, I'm sure. He would always speak well. There was nothing in the world, I heard him say once, that thrilled him as completely as a speech well-given.

I never heard him speak politically. But I sat through, I'm sure, a hundred toasts, and twice that many jokes and stories. Kikes, Polacks (Wensceslaus the Polack-kike), Canucks, traveling salesmen, Eskimo women with oversized breasts, birdies and bogeys and record trout on barbless hooks.

You could feel his power a room away. The way he played pauses and tone changes, how his voice dropped in the flat parts to build intrigue, the eye-locks he made, then broke, like a hypnotist's hand-clap. He never went for a laugh he didn't get. Or a tear either, probably, though that was never his speciality with the audiences I knew.

He had a real gift. He would go on, beginning a decade later, to capture eight elections in sixteen years without a single close contest. And in every one of them, he'd have told you himself, his real foe was the ghost of FDR.

He was an Ahab that way. He could nurse an obsession as passionately as anyone I ever knew. It was the root of his power. Take away the hate—beginning with Roosevelt, then the niggers, the kikes, and all the rest—and you had a politician without a platform. A man with only a mirror to rail at.

Nine

Billy had been a husband eighteen months when he took his first job, as a broker-trainee, in the firm of—who else?—the family of a Yale classmate. He began in January 1929, ten months before Black Thursday. All his life, his luck would be as rotten as the cards he'd deal himself.

He did well enough, I guess, for a freshman broker in the early Depression. His employer, according to his father's record of it, "refers to him as keen, greatly liked, with a quick mind, an indefatigable worker. . . . Raised from $35 to $100 a week, plus commission."

He was gone inside of four years, perhaps less. It may have been for lack of work; it was a small firm, and there weren't many orders on Wall Street in the early thirties.

Then there was some jumping around: three firms in five years, each of them rating a single-line entry in the *Yale Alumni News*. Beyond that, and some archival mentions in brokerage journals of the day, there is no record of his time at any of them.

I doubt, though, that he lost much sleep over his prospects. For a Wall Street Ivy Leaguer in the early 1930s, the times may have been jittery, but the rebound was sure to be coming; there was a lifetime to wait and lots of company in the meantime.

"It was a time when Wall Street still claimed the chosen youth of the nation," John Brooks writes in his rich and readable account of the crash period, *Once in Golconda*. Brooks is speaking of the late twenties, the months just prior to October '29, though his description is every bit as apt for the several years that followed. It would take more than a single nosedive to reverse the expectations of a generation of college boys:

> The bright boys from the best colleges went there to be lawyers or bankers, because that was the way one got rich and carved out a career. . . . The dull boys from the same colleges, the well-born athletes and playboys, pleasant-mannered, socially at ease, intellectually incurious and indolent, drifted there because it was the natural thing to do and was also the easiest place for them to make a living . . . all one needed was good customers, and for good customers there were always one's relatives and the well-heeled acquaintances one had made at school and college. Like Nick Carraway, one did not consider business hours the important part of one's life. It was in the evenings, at the long, long parties in New Jersey or on Long Island, that one really came to life, to stay up until three or four in the morning and then catch just enough sleep to make it possible to drowse through another day downtown. . . .
>
> The key to success in stock trading was exclusive information, and the distribution of such information was arranged, informally but nonetheless carefully, along social lines. There was Metropolitan Club information and Links Club information, there was even Harvard-Yale-Princeton information

and Williams-Amherst information, and a possessor of any such information would no sooner give it to someone outside his own circle, or withhold it from someone inside, than a Mafia man would betray a colleague to the police. . . .

To work in the small town south of Fulton Street in those years was to have the possibility of meeting, if not of becoming, the great of one's time or of a time soon to come. . . .

It was the mid-thirties. The Depression by now was winding down, at roughly the same pace as my father's marriage. By the fall of 1937, both were about played out. He was thirty-three, a lapsed husband and father—his two sons, ages four and eight, lived now with their mother on East Seventieth Street, where he visited on weekends—a broker at White Weld, and the proud new owner of a seat on the New York Stock Exchange.

It was his most exalted possession. He'd bought it (or somebody had bought it for him, possibly his mother) three years earlier, in July 1934, no doubt believing that the price was a steal. The cost of a seat had dropped by then to a median level of $130,000, down from a pre-Crash high of $625,000.

But his timing was as lousy as ever. Over the next six years, an average Wall Street seat would lose close to two-thirds its value; it would be twenty-five years before prices would return to post-Depression levels.

He was living alone in an apartment in the East Fifties, spending a lot of time with Yale friends and even more with a young woman named Kay, who was thinner and prettier than his wife, and had more money. It would be two more years before his divorce was final, but he was a husband in name only.

"Your father had good friends, quite a few of them, of both sexes. He was a good friend himself," Cynthia Crocker remembers. "He was fun and witty, and of course there was that sense of humor. He could *always* make you laugh. But it was more than that. He was a dear, good friend. He cared about people. We were very close—but it was never more than that."

Cynthia Crocker—Cynthia Bangs at the time, she hadn't married yet—was twelve years younger than my father. They were family friends, fellow New Yorkers, connected by ski vacations in Quebec, summers in the Adirondacks, and fathers who traveled in the same circles.

"He called me 'Baby Sis.' Then it got to be just 'Sis.' We saw a lot of each other, sometimes alone, sometimes with other people. It was like that then, a smaller world. Everybody, the whole bunch who'd gone to school together—the *right* schools, you understand—we stayed in touch, we saw each other.

"People got jobs that way, went through life that way. You had bankers who'd never banked, brokers who'd never brokered—but it was all right really, it was all among friends.

"If it was an occasion with Archie and I, we might do El Morocco. You *did* El Morocco in those days, you didn't just go there. It was the place then, you know.

"Most of the time, though, we went to smaller places, cheaper, cozier places scattered around the city. One of them, I remember, was called LaRue. Off Madison, I think, in the Fifties or Sixties. It was one of Archie's favorites—good food, good music. He always liked good music, though as I remember, he didn't care much for dancing. . . .

"There was another place. I don't remember the name—that was, what, sixty years ago? A small nightclub, I think, somewhere on the East Side. It had this colored woman, this black blues singer, who used to sing 'Loch Lomond' with such sweetness. Your father loved her. He'd always want to go there, sometimes just for one drink, just to hear her sing that song. It was a special place for him.

"My father was *so* fond of Archie. He had this name he called him—'the middle-aged reprobate.' Partly, I guess, because he was so much older than me, although that wasn't so unusual in those days. And anyway, there was never any romance between us. The real reason was something else. . . .

"My father used to make us all sign in when we came home at night—whatever kids were in the house—on this little pad he kept on the downstairs hall table. The rule was, the last one in would bolt the door.

"Well, I was always the last one, because your father would get me home so late. . . .

"And that's how the name happened—'the middle-aged reprobate.' And after a while your father would just sign 'M.A.R.' on the pad in the hall. . . .

"We had such fun together, such good, good times."

One weekend night, in the late fall or early winter of 1937, my father was invited to a party at the Bangs', a two-story red-brick town house in the East Sixties between Madison and Fifth. He'd been living as a bachelor for some months now—had returned not long ago from an autumn jaunt through the French wine country with his thin and pretty friend Kay.

The trip had been a bust—"their swan song," Cynthia Crocker calls it today—and he was again at loose ends. Yale friends, platonic dates, all-night card games, weekend visits with his sons. Waiting, always hopefully, for something to happen.

It must have been a large party. There were at least several guests my father didn't know. One of them was a beauty: thin and striking, a chain-smoking brunette of twenty-three with brown, limpid eyes, a husky, come-hither voice ("the sexiest voice you've ever heard," her brother-in-law recalls today), and an ardor for mixed company.

She was a model in the fur department at Bonwit's, a former

Farmington girl—with several classmates among the party guests—and a regular at the Bangs'. They were introduced. My father was intrigued, then smitten. Her name was Ellie Reed.

"I never thought they had much in common, really," Cynthia Crocker says. "He was so much older, you know. More serious, more worldly than your mother. He'd *lived* more. I guess that was most of it. But she was nuts for him, right from the start.

"I think he represented stability to her—I know that sounds strange, considering what happened. But I'm sure that was part of it.

"And he was so taken by *her,* her beauty, her energy. And she was nice. Your father always liked nice people."

The first dozen roses arrived within days.

"Miss Reed—With the most respectful compliments of Mr. Douglas (that middle-aged reprobate)." After that, from what I can tell, my mother never really had a chance.

She was just a girl. As coddled and adrift as my father, and ten years younger. She knew nothing of life or love, except that they both seemed—so far—to be easy, sometimes more easy than fun.

She was a peacock: showcased routinely, in ball gowns and flannel frocks, on the society pages of the *Post* and *Journal and American* ("society model," "prominent society girl," "debutante daughter of . . ."), a regular at the St. Regis roof, the Plaza, the Stork Club, El Morocco.

Men were her touchstone. She measured herself in their attentions, and by that measure she was at least a starlet. Howard Hughes dabbled with her; Serge Obolensky, the Russian playboy-predator, squired her for a season. An "innocent affair" with the fur buyer at Bonwit's got her minks at a discount. A transatlantic romance with a Belgian businessman was as close as she'd come to the real thing.

But it had been five years since Farmington. She was bored. Archie Douglas was a break in the pattern. Established, ambitious, attainable, American, a Yale man with roots, money, and an almost unshakable poise.

And not a sissy or a flit either, like the Yale boys she knew her own age. He was past the stage of silly hats, silver flasks in raccoon coats, rubbing knees under plaid blankets in end-zone bleachers. He had arrived. Or so it must have seemed to her.

And he was handsome—with watery blue eyes that could melt you on the spot, and more funny stories than anyone she'd ever met.

But love? I don't think so. I think she was flattered, scared, hopeful, certainly enthralled—which by the end would have the same effect—but I don't believe for a minute that she loved him. He was an icon. She would have had to love *up*.

As for my father, I guess I think he loved her. At least at first, as best he knew how. There's just no other way to see it.

She was beautiful certainly, but New York was full of beauties, most of them easy pickings for a Yale man in his mid-thirties with a handsome face, a Social Register pedigree, an heiress-mother, and a seat on the Stock Exchange. She had no money to speak of; her name, next to his, was nothing special. If he'd been after credentials, or a feather-bed, he could have done better than Ellie Reed.

But it was more than that. Cynthia Crocker is right. My father *had* lived more, and failed more. He knew already the deadness of sitting across the dinner table in a silent apartment from an unloved wife. He knew something at least of twenty-three-year-old brides, and how quickly the dreams turn to curlers and cold cream and four A.M. retching. It's hard to believe he hadn't learned anything, that he would twirl in his tracks for another pretty face.

But even that isn't the biggest reason. He was a romantic. Behind all the feigned sincerities and drunken drivel, behind even the heaviness of rank and money and his father's expectations— behind all appearances to the contrary—he needed badly to believe (as all four of his children, each in our own way, try to believe today) that life could be reduced to banjos and flowers, broken hearts and new beginnings.

He was a man who'd drag a date, night after night, to a side-street pub to hear a doe-eyed blues singer croon a Scottish ballad about lost love. And if I know anything about my father at all, I know that he shed a tear each time he heard it, and that the saucer on the piano—if there was one—was full of dollars when he left:

> *The wee birdies sing and the wildflowers spring*
> *And in sunshine the waters are sleepin',*
> *But the broken heart it kens nae spring again*
> *Though the woeful may cease from their greetin'.*
>
> *Oh, you take the high road and I'll take the low road,*
> *And I'll be in Scotland afore ye,*
> *But me and my true love will never meet again*
> *On the bonnie, bonnie banks of Loch Lomond.*

He was in love with love—though it had been years since he'd had an object for it. My mother, young, bright, beautiful, sexy, stylish, coveted by college boys and middle-aged Lotharios, brimming with the hope and energy he felt fading in himself, drew him like a siren.

He set his sights on her. And for at least the first few years— poems, pet names, telegrams, baskets of roses, trips to everywhere— he courted her tirelessly. And from the heart. He was in love.

I didn't see much of your parents toward the end," Cynthia Crocker says. "We lost touch. Those things happen. I tried to see your mother that last year, when she was in the hospital. But she wouldn't let me come. She was ashamed, I guess. . . .

"I didn't know she'd died. Your father called me out of the blue, a day or two later—it couldn't have been much more than that. He wanted me to come over. He said he wanted me to have something that had belonged to her.

"It was afternoon, I think. Your apartment was very peaceful,

The 1913 Riverdale School fourth-grade soccer team. My father is front left.

My father's senior picture
in the 1926 Yale yearbook.

My mother and my grandfather about 1916.

My mother at about age twelve.

My mother around 1930.

*My mother as
a model around 1937.*

At St. Agathe, Quebec, Washington's Birthday, 1938.
My mother, second from the left, is flanked by Bobby Grosjean,
far left, and my father.

My mother and father, probably at St. Agathe in 1938.

My mother and I around 1945.

My father's legislator publicity
picture around 1950.

The three of us around 1946.

*My father and I
at Massey Lake around 1946.*

Granny and Grandfather Douglas in the early forties.

My mother and I at Massey Lake, 1950.

My first fish, Massey Lake, May 1950.

*Eleanor and I in
New York, 1952.*

*Eleanor, Nanny, and I
at Massey Lake,
September 1952.*

not a soul around. Your father was sober, very calm and sad. He may have cried a little, I don't remember. He seemed sort of in shock.

"He gave me her beaver coat. The old style, with the broad shoulders—it never looked as elegant on me as it did on Ellie, it needed her height. But I wore it anyway, for years, until it practically disintegrated. And a gold bracelet, with linked rectangles, which I still have today.

"But it was what happened next that I remember the best. It was so wonderful, I've always treasured it. . . .

"We just sat down on that bed, your father and I, and started talking about Ellie. It happened so naturally. About Ellie and Archie and Cynthia—love, friendship, the three of us. In the beginning, the way-back times, before all the horrors began.

"New York, the Adirondacks, the little farm at Brewster where your parents used to go. All the places we remembered, that we shared, that we were happy in together . . .

"And do you know, we even *laughed?* Your father remembered a time, way back at the beginning, on a fishing trip in the Adirondacks, when we'd been out in the woods together—Ellie and Archie and I, and this boy I was seeing at the time, Spider Reinhart, a wonderful guy. . . .

"The blackflies were awful that trip. Everyone was just itchy and miserable, scratching and slapping all the time. There was just no relief from them.

"Anyway, I had this gunk in my pocket that was supposed to work against bugs—it was in the days before repellent, I think. And being the perfect little lady I was, I offered it to everyone else first.

"Well, I hadn't known that the stuff burned—it was some home-grown thing, you were only supposed to put on a little at a time. And the next thing I know, there they were, the three of them, howling like banshees, tripping and stumbling over trees, in a beeline for the river.

"And in they jumped, clothes and all. . . .

"Nobody thought it was funny at the time, of course. But sitting there with your father on that bed, remembering Ellie—well, the two of us just laughed till we almost cried. . . .

"It was as if we were back at the beginning again. In the early, happy times when everything was still lovely and good, before all the sickness and misery.

"It was like he was in love with her again, right then and there, for all the awfulness they'd been through. . . ."

Ten

The Robert Reeds, of Yonkers and Nantucket, were a large, stable, well-respected, quite ordinary family of upper-middle-class standing and means. The strains were Scottish-Irish; the money was modest but old. Robert Reed was a New York bond lawyer, his wife Christine a housewife of leisure.

Their children—three boys, three girls, with an age span of twelve years—were raised mostly by a nanny, at intervals by their mother. All six attended private school: the boys at Choate, the girls at Farmington. The boys went to college, the girls did not—although one, the oldest, graduated from design school.

My mother, Eleanor ("Ellie") Reed, the third child and middle girl, was described by her mother as the "most normal" of the six. She was also the prettiest, the most athletic, and probably the brightest, with an IQ of 137. There were no clouds in sight.

So what happened? Not very much, really. Indifference, anomie, indulgence mistaken for love. But it began years before my father arrived on the scene.

Looking back, it's easy enough to see where her ruin took root. But you'd have needed a crystal ball to see it coming.

My mother's father, unlike my father's, kept no journals that I know of. His life is pieced out in sixteen lines in a thin volume of genealogy published thirty years ago by a distant cousin who never knew him.

The five children who survive him today (all but my mother are still alive), now mostly in their seventies, remember him as a distant presence in their house, well-meaning but aloof, a sufferer of migraines—like my mother after him—who squinted out from behind dark glasses at family dinners.

His marriage to my grandmother, Christine Patten Reed, who gave me dollars from her hospital bed and died when I was nine, was neither blissful nor troubled. They walked to different beats, and mostly apart.

She was an Army brat, descended from a line of colonels with service in six wars. Her grandfather, George Washington Patten, had lost four fingers against Santa Anna at Veracruz. Vital, sometimes giddy, full of the prospects of the hour at hand—much like my mother would be, before life and my father beat her down—she had little to link her with her husband's somber ways.

"I always thought it was kind of sad for her," my mother's younger sister Ruth says today. "Mother was such a happy person, so full of energy. She loved to go out, to be with people. But my father never wanted to, so they stayed home most of the time. . . . We were never close to him. He was serious, absorbed in his work. An intellectual, I suppose."

He was never much of a father. He could have paid more attention, for a start. "Mischie," the family nanny, did most of the parenting for all six children, and my grandmother did most of the rest. And he could have asked more of his daughters—the boys went to Harvard, Princeton, and Trinity.

He was kind and fair, and no doubt he loved his children, but he lived through his brain instead of his heart—which made the lesson of his life as dry as old cardboard.

It's a pity, because it was a good life. (I sound like my father: "good life," "good name," "good guts.") As a man, as a member of his class—and even, in some ways, as a parent—he was an introspective version of my father's father.

Born less than four years apart, they followed the same public paths. Both were New York City lawyers with their own firms, both at the top of their field—his was municipal law. Forward-thinking men from sturdy Christian legacies of service and slow money: medicine, the ministry, small business. They may have known each other. Their offices were minutes apart.

But he never had the vision my father's father had. Or the humanness. He was a stranger to his children.

To my mother, he may have seemed more than that. The examples he set—of rectitude, reserve, responsibility, introspection— were rejected so utterly by everything she would choose, in life and in a husband, that it's not hard to imagine there may have been some rebellion involved. Her father had hidden his light under a bushel. She would flaunt everything she had, and then some. He had been prudent; she would be reckless. Her mother had married an ascetic and been deprived. She would marry a debauchee and burn her life out in wretchedness, liquor, and pills. There's more than one way of being your father's child.

The first of the Reed line to come to this country, in 1794, was the son of a Presbyterian minister from Ireland's County Donegal. Alexander Reed, my great-great-great-grandfather, the only layman among his father's sons, settled in Washington, Pennsylvania, where he took over a general store in 1796. It would remain in the family nearly as long as his father's church in Ireland: a hundred and forty years, through four generations.

In 1806, my forebear was a founding father of Washington College (later Washington and Jefferson). Four years later he was elected first burgess of the town, and several years after that became president of its bank.

In 1827, by then a prosperous man, he purchased the mansion he would call "Maple Brow," in which were raised the next two generations of Reeds—seventeen children in all, including two storekeepers, two bankers, two ministers, a congressman, a teacher, an insurance company founder, a doctor, an editor, and three soldiers, one of whom died at Chancellorsville.

There were no fortunes made that I know of, or frontiers settled or cities built. But as a line, it is as old as either of the Douglases, and larger, and at least as rich in service and sacrifice.

My mother's father, as passionless as he may have seemed to his children, apparently cherished this heritage, and nurtured dreams of its survival. In late December 1944, six months before he died, he wrote a letter to his sons, my mother's three brothers, and mailed a copy to each, dating it "Christmas 1944." (His daughters, being daughters, didn't get such letters.)

It is a page long, typed single-spaced, detailing the contributions of "roughly three centuries of Reeds"—nearly all ministers, in Scotland and Ireland—"very real men, living by and for service."

It concludes with a sentiment as touching and nearly noble as anything my grandfather Douglas ever wrote—or my father ever hooplaed—about the honor that can come with a name. And the simple, elegant hope of preserving it:

The only point of all this is that there may be in this benighted world an aristocracy not founded on wealth, men who may from generation to generation maintain a living ideal of practical service, not confined to the ministry but generally speaking best expressed in it.

Think of it occasionally—you boys all have something of it in you—and remember that it is part of your heritage, the rarest, greatest heritage we can have. . . .

Affectionately,

Dad

If she'd been a little slower, or duller or less pretty, things might have gone easier for her in the end. But girlhood, for Ellie Reed, was a party that never slowed down. There were no serious challenges, and she sought none.

At Farmington in the early thirties, she barely studied but made up for it on tests—"I was a crammer," she would say later. She was never an A student, but B's and C's were more than good enough for a pretty rich girl with no thoughts of college or worries for the future.

She was co-captain of the basketball team, played varsity tennis, and could outrun any girl in her class. In summers, there was camp. The diving and riding medals fill a whole side pocket of her suitcase.

"Your mother was very game," George Constable remembers. Constable, a childhood friend whose family summered near the Reeds in Nantucket, is today a still-active Baltimore attorney in his late seventies. "Ellie was so open and generous, so easy to like. And always game for anything. I remember one time—just a moment really, a small moment, but it sticks in my mind.

"We were sitting in the kitchen in Nantucket—just kids, probably sixteen or so. We'd been playing '21' maybe; we did that a lot in those days. Anyway, we had this bunch of grapes. And the game was to see who could get more grapes in their mouth at one time. . . .

"Well, I remember stuffing grapes into Ellie's mouth—stuffing and stuffing until her mouth was so full her eyes were popping out.

And still she wanted more. There wasn't room in there for a single other grape, and still she tried for more. . . .

"Thinking of her today, somehow—I'm not really sure why—that's the picture that comes to mind, of Ellie in the kitchen at sixteen, her eyes bulging and her mouth full of grapes. . . .

"Those were happy times we had those summers. Your mother—she knew how to have fun."

A Farmington roommate, asked to describe my mother's school-age interests, replies in a single word: "Boys." There was one, she recalls, "Worthy Johnson, his pictures filled a whole wall of the room. But there were others, lots of others, before and after."

She graduated in June of '32. By December, she was a model, appearing—"décolleté"—in a crepe ball gown at a New York benefit dinner. Fashion shows followed in New York, Boston, and Miami. She became a staple of the photo wires, with "candids" almost weekly on the society pages: "strolling" Fifth Avenue, boating in Yonkers, "passing the season" in Bermuda.

By 1935 she'd arrived—full-page spreads in *Harper's Bazaar* and the *Times* magazine. Then a screen test with MGM, and an acting contract: $150 a week to start, escalating to $1,000. I don't think she ever signed it, but it must have put the finishing touches on her ego.

New York society in the mid-thirties was a rich pasture for a society model in search of the high life. Prohibition had just been repealed, the Depression was easing. The clubs, hotels, and former speakeasies—"21," the Stork Club—were thriving as they never would again. Cole Porter was having his way on Broadway, a teenage Ella Fitzgerald was launching a career in Harlem, the Village was suddenly chic.

And in the pages of the *Journal and American,* Cholly Knickerbocker was churning out fifteen hundred words at a pop about the loves and lusts of the "café society" he claimed to have invented.

My mother twirled giddily between two worlds. Birthrighted to one, arriviste in another. Neither one fulfilled her.

In her suitcase the worlds converge. Graduation photos of college boys and Farmington classmates, eight-by-ten glossies of bridesmaids in pale gowns and après-skiers with glasses raised; press clips of new debutantes, a season pass at a Quebec ski resort, a "Volunteer Service Award" from the United Hospital Fund. The world of her sisters.

And the other, overlaid: Stork Club matchbooks, Cholly Knickerbocker columns ("No sooner had Enzo Fiermonte sailed away to Europe than the Fifth and Park Avenue sector buzzed with the rumor that . . ."); curled snapshots of middle-aged Romeos with world-weary gazes, the announcement of an "Epicurean Dinner" at the Tree Club on East Fifty-fifth ("where 'Zito' will sketch or caricature you or your friends"). A cardboard-backed photo of my mother, the perfect little vamp, being romanced at the bar of Sloppy Joe's in Havana by a white-suited sot easily twice her age.

The café crowd—the fast-track set, reliving the derring-do of Prohibition.

She wanted it all, and got it. A weekend in Greenwich with a Princeton date would be followed by a whirlwind of three A.M. nights with the gossip-column set. She'd tear out of a fashion shoot to make a football game in New Haven. Bermuda with a former classmate in the spring, a wild week in Havana two months later. It's hard to believe she ever said no to anything.

She had a cohort. Jane Holland, Farmington '32: rich, beautiful, well-born, fellow traveler, best friend, co-adventurer, comrade on the edge. And as doomed as my mother, though she would suffer nearly twice as long: four marriages, several breakdowns, one suicide attempt, a lifetime of alcoholism, purpose-searching, and abuse.

They were inseparable. At Farmington, with a third friend, they'd called themselves "the Black Bitches"—dark-haired heartbreakers, sirens at seventeen. In New York in the mid-thirties, now at the peak of their powers, they pushed every night to its last gin rickey, every man to distraction. They traveled endlessly— Bermuda, Europe, Cuba, Guatemala. They broke hearts.

From the mayor of Guatemala City, to my mother, fall 1936:

Dearest Miss Reed:

. . . You are such a lovely girl that I envy the boys that must be near you now. . . .

Is there a chance to ask you to think of me just a little while? You really cannot imagen how happy I would feel. . . . I hope that you will send me your picture. Don't forget that it will make me dream all this time until I realize my dream. That is when I be able to see you again.

Please excuse me for disturbing your attention, and acept the sincerley love that have inspire me.

Your friend the toor guide of Guatemala,

Ramon

Jane Holland died several years ago of emphysema. "Her lungs like lace" from smoking, her sister says today. I never knew her, though her life and ways were such a mirror of my mother's that I feel as though the two were one.

Two sisters survive her. One of them, the youngest, spent the summer of '36 in Europe with my mother and Jane. They sailed from New York to Le Havre, on the *Manhattan,* with the U.S. Olympic team.

"A mad, crazy trip. One of the swimmers, Eleanor Holm [the 1932 100-meter backstroke winner], got so drunk they kicked her off the team. And there was some man—another athlete, I think— running around stark naked. They put him in the brig. . . .

"Your mother and Jane, they were as wild as anyone. Not much good as chaperones, I can tell you that."

But her recollections don't stop with that trip. And none of the rest are nearly as frivolous.

"Their values were not good ones for happiness. They were so beautiful and rich and spoiled—fashionable, in-the-world, beaus and lovers and goings-out and nightclubs. So powerful. Their beauty was their power.

"It was all right when they were young. Nothing could touch them. But as they got older, it turned to disaster. . . .

"They wanted so badly, so desperately, to *be* somebody. And they could have been anything, absolutely anything. It was such a waste. It's hard to say just what went wrong. They drank too much, of course. And they seemed to want *everything*.

"I'm looking at a portrait of my sister now—as a little girl—as I talk to you. It's so very sad, so tragic. Such an awful waste."

Eleven

I like to think it might have gone differently for her. Some better timing at the beginning, a close call reversed near the end, and she might be a handsome old dowager today, closing in on her eightieth year, puttering about her perennial garden in Greenwich or Wilton or Short Hills.

It's at least possible. The world is full of faded beauties who live in peace with their memories and their liver spots.

She tried, in short, mostly futile bursts, to find some meaning that might sustain her. Some larger purpose beyond the next day's fashion shoot or next weekend's dress ball. She sketched, she wrote poetry. She took literature courses at Columbia to fill her days. She put in six hundred hours as a "gray lady" at several New York hospitals, earning for her efforts a handsome gold lapel pin with a white cross on a blue background. It went into the suitcase, still pinned to its jeweler's cardboard backing: "Robert Stoll, Incorporated, 70 Fulton St., NYC."

She was a sensitive photographer, and would fill two albums with corner-mounted black-and-white shots of Guatemalan peasant women, Irish street scenes, Nantucket boat races, ski weekends at St. Agathe. She wrote articles on "women's subjects," and submitted them regularly to Condé Nast:

> For a small weekly charge per hundred garments, one of those attractive little blue trucks with the baby and the stork on it will call at your house every other day to collect and deliver Baby's private laundry. This insures a regular supply of "didies," and also takes care of knit bath towels, wash cloths . . .

Most of her submissions were rejected ("From its treatment, it sounds a little too much like an advertisement for our purposes"). At least one, a short piece on jewelry repair, was bought by *Vogue* for four dollars in December 1934. She had just turned twenty. Perhaps she felt on the brink of a higher calling.

When in doubt, she traveled. Not always to chic destinations, and not always in style. Away from home, it seems, she was driven less by breeding than instinct.

The photo record of a 1936 trip through Central America, laid out over seven neatly spaced pages in her album, includes only a smattering of the requisite tourist shots: a temple front in Antigua, the beach at Mazatlán. Most of the rest are of life being lived: a wizened, wretched-looking street vendor in Guatemala City, a teenager approaching down a dirt street between thatch huts, some washerwomen scouring pots.

One page of the album, free of photos, is devoted to her descriptions of the land, history, and culture of Guatemala. In labored, block-print lettering—white opaque ink on a black background—she records her impressions:

> . . . Tropical lowlands rich with bananas, then the sugar plantations and the well-kept coffee lands. Blue cones of volcanoes ring the horizon, and at an altitude of 4000 feet, Lake

Amatillan stretches—a sudden sheet of blue water, bordered with hot springs and fringed with hyacinths . . .

It was on one of these trips—the same one Jane's sister remembers, to Europe in the summer of 1936, aboard ship with the drunken Olympians—that my mother met the man who almost won her.

They were shipmates. His name was Bobby Grosjean, a Belgian food company executive four or five years her senior, slim and handsome, with wavy, receding brown hair and cheeks that dimpled deeply when he smiled. They met in the cocktail lounge, a day or two out of New York.

Bobby, in his mid-eighties today and living in Brussels, recalls his first sense of her: "She sparkled. So full of energy, so beautiful to look at. And such a lovely body in a swimsuit. I was completely struck."

What began at sea continued on land. For most of the next four weeks, Bobby and my mother, accompanied off and on by Jane and her sister, biked the back roads of England and Wales—staying nights at youth hostels and country inns—visited monuments and battlefields, shared countryside picnics, woke early, stayed up late, and tried hard to make the hours last.

"She was easy to be with," he remembers. "Easy to talk to. And always ready for anything—a bike ride, a car trip, a walk in the country in the rain. Anything you wanted to do, any place new or different, Ellie was ready to give it a spin.

"And curious. She was curious about everything. She used to keep me up all night with questions about European history. Especially Waterloo. She was fascinated by it, made me tell her everything I knew."

But there was another side, too:

"She was always *pushing*—always wanted more and more and more. If it was one or two in the morning and I thought it was time to drop her home, she would want to stay a bit longer—one last cigarette, one last drink. On our bike trips together, she was never ready to stop for the day. It was always 'one more town,' 'one more hour down the road.' . . .

"She *lived hard,* she liked to live hard. Nothing was ever enough for her. . . .

"I was in love with your mother. I wanted to marry her. I wondered sometimes, though, what kind of life we would have together."

Their month ended in Paris, the night before she was to sail for home.

"We were in Harry's Bar. It was very late, we'd drunk more than we should have. Neither of us, I suppose, wanted the time to end. . . .

"In those days, you know, boys and girls didn't go to bed together so easily. I hadn't slept with your mother, and I never did after that. But that night, after we left Harry's, we went back together to the hotel—the Westminister, on the Rue de la Paix, where we all were staying, your mother and I and the others—and she came with me to my room, and that was the night we slept together. The only time. I put her on the boat the next morning."

It was July 1936. For twenty-seven of the next twenty-nine months, the Atlantic would stretch between them, a rebuke to their passions. And after that it wouldn't matter. But for most of those two and a half years, Bobby and Ellie struggled fitfully to keep the fires alive.

Letters, cables, postcards, sometimes two or three a week, swung wildly between ardor and coyness. Proposals of marriage prompted issues of fidelity: "But my darling, I have no claim on you."

Ellie's entreaties for a life in New York—"You couldn't work in the patent and engineering department *here,* then later be transferred back to Europe?"—drew frilly depictions by Bobby of the glories of the Continent: "a small hotel in Switzerland, a cruise in the summer, the States in the fall . . ."

They saw each other, on average, a month a year, in two-week stretches—each time, as Bobby would lament, "on your side of the pond." There were weekends in Woodstock, Nantucket, St. Agathe, and Mont Tremblant, long visits with the Reeds in Yonkers, some gay nights in New York. And always, everywhere, there were parties.

"Your mother was a party girl. Fascinated by that life she was living, the New York party life, until she realized how depressed it made her, and you know what happened then. . . .

"I don't think she had anything special to live for, really. She just went pillar to post. We used to talk sometimes about the idea of her getting a real job, something she could find some meaning in. . . ."

"My darling, where *am* I?"—my mother pleaded wretchedly toward the end, in the draft of a letter she'd written him but was too confused or ashamed ever to mail. Even then, she was adrift.

"What alternative have I? I'm not particularly intrigued by 'careers for women,' and I get a good deal of at least momentary pleasure out of [my life]—though that is more than counterbalanced by the dissatisfaction I so often feel. . . ."

Bobby stayed the course. He was in love—it was his way. Back in London between his twice-a-year courtship whirlwinds, he toiled valiantly, in twelve- and sixteen-page letters, written sometimes over days, to avert the extinction he must have known was coming:

When I moved into the apartment, I wished that you were there with me—to help me unpack, show me where to hang your picture, light the first woodfire. . . .

But you are in the States and I am here, and that fact is penetrating more and more. . . . Sometimes I wish that I had slept with you on that farewell night of February 20th, and that later on you could have sweetly (!) whispered in my ear that as an Armistice Day present you were to present me with a bouncing bastard. . . .

Au revoir, my love. I would prefer Europe to Bermuda for your summer holiday. . . .

In March 1938, Hitler's tanks rolled into Vienna unopposed. By September, London had mobilized, war hysteria was sweeping Europe, and Bobby was an officer in the Belgian reserves. Though he was released within days—the real battle for Belgium wouldn't come for two more years—the tone and theme of his letters to Ellie would never be the same. There was an urgency now; the coyness was gone. In its place were the bluntness, impatience, and sometimes anger of a young man who has held his tongue too long. The prospect of war had given him focus. He spoke his mind:

Last week the whole town went beserk, not due to the fear of war, but because they couldn't conceive that a whole civilization could be blown apart by the fanaticism of a single s.o.b. . . .

Ellie, my darling, I wish that for just one short moment we could both be locked up somewhere thousands of miles from the scenes of London gas mask fitters. . . .

Probably I have loved you more than I have ever loved or will ever love anyone . . . there are feelings inside of you and me which you can try and fight, and the more you fight the deeper they get, until they burst out. . . .

I once loved your provocativeness, and thought it fun to play the game with you. Pernod and a drive to Cherbourg proved my mistake. . . .

When I missed you, my love, it was more as a woman than as a [future] wife. The difference doesn't have to be so great, but it exists—and in your sometimes difficult-to-understand sense of pilgrim morality, you never liked that. . . .

Leaving Brussels at dawn was quite a sight—thousands of women around the barracks, some crying, some looking ahead as if not knowing what was going on. . . . I wonder if on that Tuesday and Wednesday there was a single girl in Brussels, London or elsewhere who didn't surrender the services of her arms, kisses and body. . . . At such moments one thinks of a lot of things, and perhaps of one or two people. I thought of you, my dear. . . .

Perhaps his brazenness scared her. Perhaps—probably—her "pilgrim morality" balked at the sudden, ungilded sexuality of his letters. Whatever the case, his passions had arrived too late. The time of Bobby and Ellie was nearing an end.

Already, her responses to his letters had grown fewer and briefer. They told of weekends in Greenwich and all-night parties on the St. Regis roof. She sent him matchbooks from the Stork Club and studio proofs from her latest modeling jobs. In one of her last letters, written in the summer of '38 in a daze of giddiness you can almost touch as you read it, she confessed to her brief winter fling with Serge Obolensky:

"Slight but typical," she wrote with a candor that swung between apology and pride. "Every girl has to go through it once."

But she was fooling no one. Least of all herself. It had been six years since her debutante season; the café crowd was turning over, old beaus were starting families, the Black Bitches were now young wives. There was war in the air.

The band had stopped playing, but Ellie was still twirling—an overage ingenue rote-stepping to the only beat she knew on a floor that was darkening as she danced. For the first time in her life, she doubted her powers. She was scared, though by the time she glimpsed the dangers, they were upon her.

Sometime in the summer or early fall of 1938—in the same letter-draft to Bobby she was too ashamed to mail, dated only "Monday Nite"—she wrote as follows:

One day I decide I'm very much in love with you, and the only thing in the world I want is to be with you always and try to make you happy—and then, Bobby, I think that perhaps it wouldn't be fair to marry you as I'd only make you desperately unhappy. . . .

I've been running around a lot since you left. To confess, in confidence, Archie Douglas . . .

I know I'm living a foolish, futile existence. Oh, Darling, this is more of a mess than you realize. . . .

It was Bobby, in the end, who gave out first. The letter arrived in Yonkers a day or two after Christmas 1938:

. . . The girl is an American whose father works in Brussels [as U.S. ambassador to Belgium]. I've known her quite a long time, and until recently she was never more to me than just a very agreeable and sweet friend. This fall, with the crisis and its anti-climax, I felt sad, lonely and unhappy looking for something concrete to lean on. And that is how it started. . . .

"What *else* could I do?" he asks today, more than half a century later, over the phone between Brussels and Boston. His question, it seems to me, is only half rhetorical.

"I loved her, I would have married her. But I lived on this side, she lived on that—and my life, I think, never appealed to her anyway. She was so much the party girl. . . .

"And everything, with your mother, was such a yo-yo game. So emotional, always up and down. You never knew where you stood with her. . . .

"And then she met your father—and that was the end of it."

Twelve

The first picture of my father that appears in my mother's album was taken over Washington's Birthday weekend of 1938, at St. Agathe, Quebec.

They are sitting together in a horse-drawn sleigh, their skis and poles stuck upright in front of them. My mother is wrapped and hooded in fur, her face partly hidden, a lap robe over her knees. He is next to her in a tan greatcoat, bareheaded and serene, staring soulfully at the camera. The horse's rump and tail are visible in front of them, as is their driver, an old man in a dark wool cap and mittens, a cigarette at the corner of his mouth. The sleigh is tiny and delicate, with a curved wooden prow and runners that finish in a flourish at the back. There is snow everywhere, a stand of birches in the background. It is a wonderful picture.

But there is a second image of that weekend. A group shot this time: twelve après-skiers—four men, eight women, Jane and Cynthia among them—standing in the snow, drinks in hand, outside the Laurentide Inn on the afternoon of February 20. It is a festive shot. My mother is second from the right, with my father next to her. On her other side, their shoulders touching, one hand in his pocket and the other around a glass of beer, is Bobby.

It was the last weekend he would spend with her, the weekend of their "farewell night" and the "bouncing bastard" that never was. He would sail for London the Tuesday after it ended, and would see her next—eleven months later, in January 1939—only long enough for a stormy good-bye.

I don't know what my father was doing there that weekend. He'd known Ellie three or four months by then, since the night of the party at the Bangs' town house. Perhaps Cynthia had invited him—she is standing to his left in the picture, a male arm around her shoulder. Or perhaps my mother had, thinking that Bobby would have sailed by then. However it happened, he had to have known there were risks involved—upstaging another man's last thunder, forcing the issue as odd man out.

But that was his style. He was a plunger. Gutsy, theatrical, cocky, impetuous, never a man to wait his turn. He must have sensed that Bobby's time was ending, that there was nothing to be lost by granting him his swan song. But that wasn't his way.

For my father, the best defense, always, was a bold offense. You pressed, you bullied, you forced your will—but smiling every step of the way, holding eye contact, keeping your handshakes firm. And in the end, they loved you for it. Or if they didn't, they couldn't say just why. Win or lose, you came out clean.

"Your father was always agreeable to be with," Bobby says today, still gracious after all these years. "I remember sitting around the fire with him, just chatting and bulling, nothing very serious. . . . I knew he was attracted to your mother—so were other men, she was spoiled by men. But what could I do? I just hoped that nothing would come of it."

Such a man, when it came to the winning of Ellie Reed's heart, could be no match for my father. She wanted dash, not chivalry— to be won, not waited for. She wanted Rhett Butler. She was a fool, and at least part of her knew it.

"I'm such an idealist," she wrote Bobby toward the end, at the height of her confusion, "to think that a man should be the sun, the moon and all the stars to me."

By the time he found his feelings and tried to rise to them ("I wish I had slept with you," "there are feelings inside you . . ."), the cause had already been lost. And for Bobby at least, it may have been just as well. His Brussels lady-love, soon to be his wife, would raise four children with him and share half a lifetime before they were divorced in the early seventies. He could have done worse.

As for my mother, it's hard to be as sanguine. She loved Bobby— not dangerously enough to suit her hell-bent tastes, but with a depth and realness she was wise enough to see.

"I have more respect and sane adoration for you than I've ever had for anyone," she wrote him in the summer of '38, in the same never-mailed draft in which she confessed to her affair with my father.

"I can't be a have-my-cake-and-eat-it-too girl all my life. Oh darling, I wish your job could have sent you back here. I wish so much it could be different for us."

Why did she keep that draft? By what divining, late-night instinct did she store it—twice folded, half-finished, barely legible—in the suitcase with her treasures and her charms? And then never, for fifteen years after, take it out?

And what if she'd mailed it? What if she'd let him know how scared she was, how close he was to winning her? Might he have been bolder sooner? Might there have been a "bouncing bastard"? Might she be seventy-eight today?

My father, with Bobby safely back in London, pressed his cause. It couldn't have been easy. A still-married man of thirty-four, the father of two small children, didn't bull his way into the life of a twenty-four-year-old New York darling, no matter what her fears. The Obolensky thing came and went about that time—late spring or early summer of '38—and a man named John from Philadelphia who kept inviting her to parties that she only sometimes turned down. And Jane, who never liked my father to begin with, and would grow to loathe him by the end—Jane was a fan of Bobby's from the start.

And there was still Bobby. A dying force, but not yet out of mind. It had been two years. There was strength in that.

Even so, my father must have known he had her won—that it was only a matter of time. He was a careful judge of weakness. He had to see her restlessness, her panic, how needy she was for something more grounded than a modeling career that would end with the first wrinkle.

And if there was anything he could offer, it was that. He was a Douglas—moneyed, Wall Street–connected, son of an heiress, cousin to a congressman. His mother was a member of the Colony Club, his father of the Century, the Union League, and St. Andrew's. There was an apartment on Park Avenue, an estate in the Bronx, a farmhouse in the country, a camp in the Adirondacks. Trust funds large and certain. The family's rugs were Persian, the silver Tiffany. The men caught brook trout on their grandfathers' bamboo rods. Things were done a certain way. It mattered how you said good morning.

"Ellie was very conscious of the Douglas name," Cynthia Crocker remembers. "Very impressed by it. Your family had such great, great pride in its name. Over time, I guess, she just took that on. Before long, she began talking like your grandmother—'We're going *oot*.' "

It was more than his name, of course. He was handsome: lean face, jutted jaw, liquid blue eyes, straight dark hair that would gray early. He had political ambitions—she could see herself, no doubt, as a senator's wife. He was witty and well-liked, and had lots of stories. They made a strong doubles team.

And he adored her. Telegrams, flowers, presents, midnight hansom rides through Central Park. He went after her heart like a pirate after booty—no risk too great, no rival too tall. She liked that. It thrilled her. It was the way she wanted to be loved.

Still, she demurred. He was married—technically at least—which made decisions moot. But it was more than that. He was so sure of everything: himself, his ideas, the way the world worked. There was never room for questions with him, or for doubt. It wasn't like with Bobby. And he seemed so *angry* sometimes. She was never sure at what. He scared her a little.

And he could be so staid—a "stick-in-the-mud," she would call him later. Almost pious sometimes. He was wonderful around people, the center of every crowd. Yet he didn't like big parties, or said he didn't. And they almost never went dancing. He hated to dance, he said.

He confused her. He seemed so old sometimes.

It went on like that—him pursuing, her relenting, then resisting. A weekend in Woodstock, a dinner in New York, then she'd duck him for a week. It wasn't hard, at least at first. There were other men, other invitations, always someplace else to go. Then the flowers would arrive and it would start again.

Flowers were his medium: bouquets, corsages, single red roses, by messenger or in person, at improbable times in improbable places. They began after the Bangs' party—"the middle-aged reprobate"—and continued, at intervals, for at least the next year. They were always well-timed, though she could never predict their timing. It maddened her. But she seldom said no the next time he called.

They came, all of them, with sealed envelopes bearing tiny cards. The words were never many, though they were no doubt sufficient. The cards are undated, though it isn't hard to infer, at least roughly, their order of delivery:

Darling: Just to officially open the early summer drinking season. Love, AD Jr.

Darling: I hope I won't have to use this same corsage again. All Love, AD Jr.

Precious Ange: With all love from your mean, disagreeable, horrid, thoughtless, but completely adoring old man.

Dearest: I love you and I am so damn disappointed. AD Jr. (Only ten days—much too much.)

Ange: We have decided that we are very much in love.

Time, in the end, was on my father's side. It was in May 1938 that Muriel Richards, the third of Farmington's three Black Bitches, had become the second to take a husband. There were eight bridesmaids. Ellie was one of two still single. It was the first of four weddings she would attend that year.

By summer her swirl with the Russian playboy had run its course. He was "more like an uncle," she confided to a friend.

In August she learned by rumor that her Philadelphia suitor had pledged his troth to a New Jersey girl.

In September she wrote Bobby proposing a trip to London. He cabled his response:

THANKS WONDERFUL PROPOSITION   CONSID-
ERING CHAOTIC INTERNATIONAL MESS BELIEVE
ADVISABLE POSTPONE TRIP UNTIL SOLVED
HOPE PEACEFUL OUTCOME   LOVE

In December came the truth: "The girl is an American. . . ."

A month later Bobby arrived in New York. They met at the home of a friend. He was engaged to be married, he told her.

She threw a typewriter at him.

Four months later she said yes to my father, pending his divorce.

("They married when it was time to marry," Jane's sister says today of the two friends. "They weren't equipped. They never understood love.")

In July 1939 my father's first wife flew to Reno. The grounds were desertion, the settlement two thousand dollars a year per child.

They were married nine months later, April 5, 1940, a Friday, at the Madison Avenue Presbyterian Church. The reception was in the Victorian Room at the Carlyle. There were fewer than eighty guests. Ellie would have preferred it larger, but it was Archie's second and the divorce had been recent. Discretion prevailed.

My Dear Ellie:

I am entrusting to you for safekeeping the enclosed check. . . .

It is idle for me to assure you that it will be with great delight that we welcome you into our family circle. To date we have all been on our very good behavior, and even when we drift into the drab level of every day, I hope you will not find us, at any time, too cantankerous or perverse.

We welcome you with joy into all our moods—whatever their gamut may be!

Till Friday then, with love and affection from us both, matriarch and patriarch.

Faithfully,
Archibald Douglas

The honeymoon was in Havana. There is a single page devoted to it in her album: two beach shots, four fishing shots, their chauffeur ("Marcelino"), the view from their hotel. But no trace of it in the suitcase, in which my father never appears again.

Archie
and Ellie

Thirteen

My mother, for all she knew, married for love at twenty-five. The union would last thirteen and a half years, nearly all of her adulthood, and for it she would spend her sanity and her life.

And yet, in her suitcase of little treasures—which she tended till the end, adding to it only weeks before her death—out of more than thirty photos, several dozen cards and letters, diving medals, bracelet charms, journals and papers, there is not so much as a snapshot to mark her marriage.

In her album there are dozens of them. She took pictures, for nearly twenty years, of anything that moved. It was a kind of self-therapy, I think. The linear, unweighted recording of her life. Needlepoint made personal.

But the suitcase was different—a storehouse of the heart. And what is there of my father—six love notes, two photos, two telegrams, the divorce agreement ending his first marriage—lapses benignly in November 1939 ("SUNDAY TRAIN LEAVES HERE 1:32 P.M.   ARRIVES HARMON 6:57   HOW ABOUT DINNER"), five months before their marriage.

After that, except for a single letter from Jane, years later, pleading with her to leave him ("You know, deep within you, there can be no happiness this way"), it is as though she had tried to purge him from her heart by expelling him from the suitcase—even as she shared his bed and bore his children—like a teenager tearing pages from a diary.

The years between 1940 and '44, between their marriage and my birth, play out in my mind as scenes cut at random from a movie, then spliced together and played back on a screen too small to contain their image. A pastiche, without rhythm or substance, even the fragments sheared off at their edges.

The pictures of these years fill half an album. Skiing in Canada, fishing in the Adirondacks, picnics at Narragansett, golf and tennis at a club in the Carolinas.

Everywhere, it seems, there were friends: scores of friends I never knew and a few I did; festive, jocular group poses on the beach, at weddings, around picnic tables, in the steam bath after skiing. Ellie giving backrubs, Archie building snowmen—the gaiety never ends. And everyone, almost always, with a glass in their hands or a bottle on the table. A grand, gaudy life, full of laughter and diversion. But barely a shot—only one out of dozens—of the two of them together.

There was a war going on. My father's Yale classmates were enlisting in droves. I don't know how he managed to stay out of it—or where he found his playmates those years.

I remember him saying once, when I was still a young boy, that he'd been "robbed of two wars"—too young for one, too old for the next. I grew up believing that he'd have been a soldier if he could have—a hero probably—that he'd been cheated by birth of the right to vent his furies against the fascism and injustice he spent a lifetime reviling. He was nearly thirty-eight when Pearl Harbor was hit; I never doubted his story.

What I didn't know was that the draft-age cutoff during the war was forty-five—and that men his age and older were enlisting every day.

He had connections, high blood pressure, a new wife, and two dependent children. I assume the answer lay somewhere in the mix. However he did it, he played through the war as he'd played through the Depression ten years before. For all his posings as a man with his finger on the pulse of the world, its affairs seemed always, somehow, to go on without him.

My mother's life, what had been left of it before her marriage, seems suddenly to have been expunged. Purged from the record as though by amnesia. A Farmington roommate recalls that she "just disappeared." Another friend, a fellow traveler through the early and mid-thirties, does not remember even knowing whom she married.

The modeling stopped. Old friends were abandoned or dropped away, the café crowd went on without her. Even Jane, after some early attempts to make her peace with my father, faded steadily into the distance.

Their friends were his. Holiday dinners took place at his parents'; the Adirondacks replaced Nantucket for vacations. She learned to shoot grouse, to cast a fly.

Cynthia Crocker, the only close friend they still shared from the early days, was a witness to this molting: "She just denied herself, that's all. More and more as time went on—her friends, her interests, all the things she loved. She wanted so badly to be a part of his life, to be a Douglas.

"It was such a shame, so difficult to watch. No one was ever more attractive in her own right."

For a time at least—three years, four, perhaps longer—my mother's recasting seems to have raised no scars. These were the years her albums are fullest of. And the years, too—overlaying the golf and skiing, the party weekends—of gentler, more prosaic things:

Furnishing a new home—their first apartment, on Fifty-seventh Street, a block west of the one I remember—learning to cook for two, getting to know stepsons, hostessing dinners with new friends.

She was a wife. And as close to happy as she would ever be again.

"They were wonderful together those years," Cynthia says today. "You'd have thought they were meant for each other. Your father was so proud of her—her beauty, her energy, all the things she did. And Ellie, she was just happy to be a part of his life. They were a joy to be around, they really were."

If there was a first sign of trouble, it would have to have been the booze. It was everywhere. It drenched their life: softened failings, created friends from strangers and—ultimately—lovers from friends, painted invincibility onto everyone it touched. And in the circles they ran in, it was as basic as air.

"It was unthinkable not to drink," Cynthia says. "Impossible to consider doing anything without it. It was an important—a necessary—part of life. And innocent, so innocent. No one thought a thing about it.

"Without the drinking, probably none of us would have been so fascinated with each other. We'd have gotten to know each other better, maybe learned some things. [As it was], there was no realness at all. Everybody called everybody else 'dah-ling,' there were lots of hugs and kisses, nothing underneath. . . .

"Part of it, of course, came from being so spoiled. We were *all* spoiled in those days—plenty of money, so much time on our hands. Or if you weren't, you pretended to be. You did that then, you did it all—the drinking, the parties—whether you could afford to or not. It was a way of life, the way of living we had. . . .

"Then suddenly, one day, you woke up and found yourself caught by it. And you couldn't expect any sympathy—people just said you were *'weak.'* That's what they called it then when someone drank too much, a 'weakness.' Especially if it was a woman—there was a double standard that way.

"Then, if it got worse—drinking for 'medicinal purposes,' blackouts, all those sorts of things—why, then they would just say you were *'nervous.'* That was the name they gave it then. Everything was 'nervous'—a 'nervous breakdown,' a 'nervous condition.' No one ever called it by its real name.

"You couldn't get any help, any understanding. So what did you do? You kept on drinking. There was nothing else to do, and everyone else was doing it. And it just pulled you down. . . .

"Oh, it wasn't just your parents, believe me. There were so many others—so many, many horrid endings I could tell you about. You don't even want to know."

Fourteen

For close to six years, through the end of the fifth year of their marriage, not a single new treasure made the suitcase. It sat in its place, on the hat shelf of my mother's closet, the lapsed record of a slowly unraveling life. There's no reason to believe she opened it once.

Then, sometime in the spring or summer of 1945, the entries resumed in a torrent. She was a mother now. Her subject was me:

Bald and toothless on my tummy in the crib, toddling on chubby little legs through the grass of an Adirondack summer; as a five-year-old, preening with my first trout in the spring of 1950, the brim of a ridiculous, oversized fishing hat—my father's—reaching nearly to the edges of my shoulders.

It's shocking, considering her paltry investment in motherhood, all the things she kept:

Valentine's Day cards, a birthday card ("Not Just for Today But Forever"), a handwritten "Happy Easter" on lined school paper; a page torn from a calendar book, dated Decoration Day, Tuesday,

May 30, 1950: "I Love You" over a pink and green drawing of what looks like a fish on feet. A note to Santa Claus: "i have been a good boy. Please may i haeve a soldier suit Hoppalong suit battery train. My babys sister wants doll carrage Love Geoffrey." This also dated—on the envelope, in my mother's hand—"1950."

After that, it seems, except for a flurry of formal toddler shots of my sister, who would arrive too late to bring much comfort, almost nothing was worth saving.

I was born July 1, 1944, twenty-five days after D-Day, at the precise midpoint of the first decisive year of my parents' marriage.

My father turned forty that January. Three weeks later, in a speech before the New York Republican Club, he announced his candidacy for a seat in the Legislature. Ten months after that, on December 29, 1944, he was sworn in by Governor Dewey to his freshman term as assemblyman for the Eighth District of Manhattan. His wife, he would say later, "because of her appearance," was his "greatest political asset."

My mother turned thirty in November, a week to the day after his election. She spent the morning of her birthday in bed alone with a migraine. She would remember it later as among the worst days of her life.

My birth had been a blow to them both. My father had counted on a daughter. He had two sons already, he had reminded his wife, and had "no use" for a third.

She had wanted badly to oblige him. Her failure, never forgiven, was the first direct hit on a marriage already blighted by liquor, boredom, and the beginnings of self-pity. For most of the four months after I was born, my father would recall later: "She was depressed, slowed down, had no interest in anything."

She did manage, he allowed, to "come out of it in time" for the final stages of his campaign.

Their circle narrowed. Even Cynthia rarely saw them now as a couple. They held their trips to one a year: Bermuda in the spring of '46, Sun Valley in '47. The ranks of revelers had been depleted by the war. They partied now mostly at home.

Bea was hired, and their dinnertimes took on a new civility. The first nanny came and went—a roly-poly Scotswoman named Jean Broadfoot with a thick brogue, an easy twinkle, and a love of children I would never know again in the parade of witches that followed. She left before I turned four, but was there at my wedding nearly thirty years later, weeping in her Scotch at the prospect of her "wee Geoffrey" taking a wife.

My mother took up decorating, and worked briefly—and part-time—on Long Island with a family friend. When that paled, she fell back for a while on her role as "gray lady," this time at Memorial Hospital, where my father—like his grandfather, father, and cousin before him—served dutifully as a director. She was bored. All her life, boredom would stalk her—a silent gray ghost.

By the fall of 1948, her efforts at purpose had largely lapsed. More and more now, she was fighting her migraines. But even when she was fit, her days focused mostly around hairdressers, fur sales, and long, wet lunches with Jane, Cynthia, her sister Ruth, or the wives and sisters of her husband's Yale friends. She was at sea. And it would only get worse.

My father was "Honorable" now—a member of the Assembly's Conservation and Ways and Means committees, the Ivy Republican Club, the First Avenue Boys' Association, the St. Nicholas Club, the Pilgrim Society. By 1948 he had been the sponsor of at least two bills—on child welfare and hospital funding—and was vice commissioner of the state's Legislative Committee on Rents. Headwaiters lavished him, speeding tickets were dispatched with a quip and a smile ("We work for the same boss, Officer"), his face—

"Honest, Sincere, Conscientious"—peered down from billboards for weeks at a time.

In the parched little world of the Upper East Side, he was a Somebody. By the early fifties, though nothing would come of it, he would be talking freely about running for Congress.

As a broker, he was set for life. Or so it must have seemed. His employer, since the late thirties, had been the same: Pershing & Company, 120 Broadway. Its principal was Jack ("Persh") Pershing, son of General Jack Pershing, conquering hero of World War I.

Persh and Archie had some things in common: Both were Yale men, both skied and golfed avidly, and both had chosen their brides from among the three Black Bitches of Farmington's class of '32.

Persh and "Mo-Mo" are regulars in my mother's album: at Rhode Island outings, Adirondack picnics, Jane's sister's wedding in the summer of '40, the slopes at St. Agathe.

The last photo of them—"Dunes Club, Narragansett, July '47"—was taken at the beach on a cloudy day. Mo-Mo, in a wide straw hat and bright bathing suit, leans languidly against Persh, who smiles out at the camera, a drink in his hand. My father sits nearby, one leg splayed across a striped beach towel, the other on the sand, also drinking.

It wasn't long after that that Archie would become an embarrassment—then a source of sadness—to his friend and boss. The gay weekends wound down, then ended. But he would stay on at Pershing through the rockiest of times, and Persh's loyalty, however strained, would last another decade.

I remember next to nothing of these early times: a small bedroom with pale walls in an apartment that is otherwise a blank to me, some flashes of Bea and Jean Broadfoot, a colored Easter egg peeking out from behind a curtain in what must have been the spring of my fourth year.

My sister was born that same month—April 1948—and we moved a block east, to the western fringe of Sutton Place, the apartment of the childhood I remember, where the nannies came and went in a blur of white dresses, my parents swooped and faded—swooped and faded—like movie cowboys, and the silence was a prison without bars.

I entered kindergarten, at The Church of the Heavenly Rest on Ninetieth Street and Fifth Avenue, in September of 1949. I remember a large room with close-set desks, a plaid blanket robe I kept stored in a cubby in the corner except at rest times, and the smell of the teacher when she bent over my desk, which made me think of air freshener. My best friend there—the *only* friend I remember—was a prankish, curly-haired boy named Jock Chamberlain, who would follow me through two more schools, though never again as much of a friend. I was invited sometimes, on weekends, to his apartment for the night, though he never came to mine. No friend came to mine, in all the years we lived there. Between my mother's constant migraines and my father's dread of "snivel-nosed brats," it would have been unthinkable to ask.

"In almost every respect, Geoffrey is ready for First Grade work next year," my teacher wrote in her final report in the spring of 1950:

It is apparent, however, that he will need guidance during the summer to help him build a more secure emotional state so that he can adequately approach the formal work. At present he is completely dependent on mood for success. . . .

This erratic behavior is obviously caused by an emotional disturbance on Geoffrey's part which is interfering with his natural intelligence. We feel that with careful help and encouragement Geoffrey may be ready in the fall to do the good work of which we are sure he is capable.

I would never do good work—or even half-good work—though it would be another thirteen years before an "emotional disturbance" was ever again cited as the reason. And by that time, its causes were history.

I was not an easy child. I swallowed quarters, threw water bombs—and HELP! notes—out my window, kicked my nannies, bullied my sister, and lied about everything. At six, I developed a compulsion that lasted nearly two years and ravaged whatever small tolerance my father still had of me:

Any object small and blunt enough that neither melted, rotted, burned, nor smelled—spitballs, eraser bits, pencil leads, a miniature Chinese checker—I would jam as deeply into my ear canal as I could manage, tamping it in each time with the butt end of a pen or pencil, then testing its depth by dripping water into my ear to assure that I had created an impassable blockage.

Never once, out of more than a dozen times, was anything ever removed by other than medical means. Twice it took surgery. On one occasion, a nonsurgical one, the doctor removing an eraser wedge from my right ear was interrupted in mid-process by a phone call; I was left alone in his treatment chair, which had a small tear in its plastic covering. I removed a bit of the sponge rubber stuffing and jammed it deeply into my left ear, using one of his instruments to complete the tamping. When he returned and had completed his removal of the eraser wedge, I asked him to check the other ear once again—"just in case."

I never understood what drove me to do this. I was honestly terrified of my father's rages—"You're *BREAKING* me, you understand? *BREAKING* me!"—and of the beatings I nearly always got. I meant it, each time, when I swore never again to repeat my folly. But each time, defying my earnestness, the promise gave way.

In the end, they made me wear gloves—at school, at home, once even to bed. The humiliation of this, coupled with the practical problem of tweezing with leather fingers, put an end to the practice. My father placed his cost at the equal of a year's tuition.

Buckley was a school for young gentlemen. There were, as far as I knew, no blacks, Jews, indigents, ethnics, or minorities of any stripe. The boys who attended Buckley went on to Groton, Andover, Exeter, Deerfield, and St. Paul's. We were boys of promise, from whom fine things were expected.

The mayor's son's desk was right behind mine. Behind him sat the son of the president of a big defense firm. There were bankers' boys and brokers' boys, and perhaps, somewhere or other in the school, the son or two of a playwright or anthropologist. We were a well-heeled lot.

I had few friends at Buckley—or any other school I went to. My dealings were mostly with the flakes and eggheads.

There was one, a red-haired boy with big lips and thick glasses, who lived in an apartment on Park Avenue even more massive than Granny's—but gaudy, so gaudy and vulgar I knew even at six he wasn't one of us—and chewed on dollar bills and had cracked, red blisters at the corners of his mouth.

And another—his name was Strange—the class genius, so wizardly he was doing algebra problems in third grade. Strange was short and skinny and as pale as a sheet, and made funny, gurgling noises with his throat. He was always smiling. Even at his desk, which was next to mine, his stubby, pushed-up nose stuck deep inside a math book, he would smile his little smile, as though at some secret joke he alone was brainy enough to fathom.

I hated him. I hated his smile. On the school bus home in the afternoons, on days before a math test, I would bend his arm back and Indian-burn his skinny wrists until they almost bled: He would let me see his test answers in class the next day, I told him, or I would do much, much worse. He never seemed frightened—he never even seemed in pain—but he did stop smiling, and he did tip his answer sheets my way.

I cheated on nearly every math test I took in third grade. It wasn't until fourth that I got caught, and it wasn't Strange who ratted on me. God bless him, wherever his smiling genius has taken him since then.

The reviews of my Buckley performance, initially at least, were mixed.

"At times Geoffrey's impulsiveness gets him into trouble," my first-grade teacher noted in the spring of 1951. "He has a quick little temper, which can flare up suddenly but never lasts long."

At the same time, she added, "He is friendly, vivacious, enthusiastic, and alert. He has completed a satisfactory year's work."

That was as good as it would get. By second grade, the academic pattern of my next fifteen years had taken root:

"Geoffrey needs to develop greater independence and maturity . . . easily distracted, oblivious to directions, very immature in relation to the group . . . noisy, jumpy, distracts his neighbors, erratic behavior, short attention span, operates usually at a high pitch. . . ."

The reactions to my report cards never varied. My father was "disgraced," my mother didn't comment. I lost my allowance for a week or a month. The weekend husbands warned me gravely about the hazards of not "toeing the line," before patting my head and handing me their quarters.

I lived for the summers. We all did, I think, though for very different reasons.

Massey Lake, on the northern fringe of the Adirondacks—twenty-six miles from the Canadian border at Fort Covington—is today a hapless little two-mile stretch of water whose shores are dotted with "bucolic" enclaves that struggle seasonally at cross-purposes. At one end is a nudist colony, at the other a camp for overweight teens. There is an "alternative" writers' workshop (Ferlinghetti is still very big here), a private "retreat" for troubled youths, and a cluster of one-room pine shanties that calls itself the "Village for Holistic Self-Governance."

By mid-September all of these are shuttered, as are the half-dozen private summer homes that remain. The only year-round residents are a family of three millionaire sisters, a retired court stenographer and her husband, and a handful of paper company employees who commute daily to nearby St. Regis Falls. All told, the winter population of Massey Lake is less than twenty-five.

But winter was never the point. Massey Lake, in the years of my childhood and teens—until its community was scattered by a spate of deaths, divorces, and unexplained fires—was a summer Eden (or Sodom, as some of my parents' crowd remember it today) of treasure hunts, tennis matches, canoe races, ghost stories around campfires stoked through the night by leather-faced old guides, three-month friendships that picked up each June precisely where you'd left them.

And in the later years: two-pound rainbows that ripped line off your reel with a sound you'd learned to dream of, costume parties that lasted till dawn, blond girls in torn sneakers who let you put your hand down their fronts for the price of a single "I love you."

Massey Lake parents were giddy and indifferent, and seldom rose before ten. Pale-faced nannies with their hair in tight buns clustered shoeless on boat docks, tittering like schoolgirls. Even the maids only barely kept house.

Massey Lake was the place of my father's summers, and of his father's and great-uncle's before him. For three-quarters of a century, since before the first beam was cut for the first summer camp sometime in the 1880s, this lake, and the lakes and rivers around it, had been where Douglases had come as children to learn to fish.

There was a pride and a permanence in that. It was part of what we grew up to know as the honor of our name.

"One of my old flybooks, frayed and beaten, what a wealth of days it recalls," my father's father reflected in his journal in the summer of his sixty-first year. "I can see every turn of every stream, hear the spring water chuckle through the flooded alders. . . ."

In 1880, at the lake head under the great rock, looking out at the stars and the moon on the water—my first night under the sky out of doors. And in 1915, with Jack and Billy, the first of many expeditions with the boys together. . . .

The changelessness of those matchless virgin forests—the lake, the river, the rapids, the runs, the ripples, under God's sky, bordered by hemlock, spruce, beech, birch, maple, and an occasional primeval pine—are abiding memories from my childhood. They are unchanged, there since my first venture in 1879. The same old trails go over the mountains, in the same pools we find trout year after year, and the high hills still silhouette the sky. . . .

But as important, bacon frying in the pan and buckwheat cakes at breakfast—the old-time joy and gusts of life and good company . . .

We arrived always after dark. I can remember the crunch of the gravel in the driveway of our camp, and my sister, asleep for hours, being lifted by my father and carried in his arms to the couch in the living room, where she would sleep another half-hour under a blanket until Nanny and my mother had had time to make the beds. And the smell of the air, so pure it seemed bottled, and the sounds of water lapping the dock in the blackness below. That first arriving moment, each early-June night, held a promise for me that was never broken.

I thought of our camp as a fortress. Twenty-foot-high cathedral ceilings of knotted pine, supported by thick, polished beams that met in a V at the peak; a stone fireplace big enough to stand in, rooms the size of whole houses, closets the size of rooms. When I grew up, I told Nanny, I would live in that camp.

We knew every family on the lake. There were only about twenty. Most, like us, lived in rambling wood palaces with high knotted ceilings, more rooms than they would ever use, and two-story boat houses with gable roofs and wide French doors on the second floor that opened onto balconies from which merrymakers, on windless nights, called to one another across a mile of lake.

Everyone was rich, some far richer than we. Most, like us, arrived in early June with carloads of maids and nannies and luggage enough for the three-month summer. (Bea came only one year. She was afraid, she said, of "woods creatures" and of nighttime noises that kept her awake. So we hired our maids out of St. Regis Falls, or from agencies in the city.) We arrived to musty, sheet-draped living rooms, blanket boxes that—nearly always—had been invaded by mice, and boat houses that quartered sailfish and sneak boxes, birch canoes, leaky gray dinghies, Adirondack guide boats that cut through the water as sleekly as sculls. And sometimes, in the richer camps, handsome, spruce-ribbed outboards with brass fittings and mahogany trim, that could take you to the end of the lake and back in the time it took to walk between camps.

Probably half the families lived in New York. Several, like the Coes, whose camp was next to ours, and the Hubbards, who were across the lake (in what is today the writers' colony), were among my parents' winter weekend crowd. Others we saw only in the summers. It never seemed to matter, though. Everyone went to all the parties.

There was one nearly every weekend night. By eight o'clock or so, on any Friday or Saturday evening when the lake was calm, you could stand out on the boat-house balcony and hear the laughter—

each peal drowning out the last, like herky-jerky birdcalls, coming over the water from half the lake away. After dark it got louder and gayer, and by then you could *see* it—or seem to see it: the longest, brightest light-pool on the water, the boat house that outshone the rest.

And the light and the laughter came together in your mind, and with it the boat house—you knew every corner of every camp on the lake—and it almost didn't matter that you couldn't be there.

Every three weeks or so—four or five times a summer, never more—it would be our turn to give the parties. These were grand times for me. There were more people than on weekends in the city (though always some of the same) and I would be allowed to stay up later, often as late as ten. There were no hors d'oeuvres to pass—at Massey Lake, for whatever reason, people helped themselves—though I would sometimes carry trays of drinks for my father from the bar, around the room to our guests.

These were the gayest parties, except for Granny's, I had ever been to. I sipped more gin from more glasses, got more kisses and quarters—and sometimes dollar bills—the jokes were freer and naughtier, the laughter louder than in New York.

"Cover up your ears, young man," my mother would tell me once or twice a night, and I would make a show of sticking my index fingers in my ears while someone told a story about breasts or bedrooms or Polish bridegrooms on their wedding night.

These were as close to family times as our family ever came, at Massey Lake or in New York. We shared no meals together, went to no ballgames, circuses, picnics, or plays. We talked rarely, and never as a family. Even on Christmas, there were guests in the house by noon.

It was as though we were afraid of ourselves—that the air might combust around us if we were left in the same room together, alone, for longer than it took to say good night.

Of all our guests in New York or Massey Lake, my favorites were the Coes. Together with the Hubbards, they were my parents' best friends. Mr. Coe and my father fished and hunted together often, and had dinner sometimes in the city without their wives. Mrs. Coe and my mother went on shopping trips to Best's and Bonwit's, and shared lunches at The Passy and the St. Regis Grill.

The Coes owned a chain of sporting goods stores in New York and New England. They had a house upstate, a camp at Massey Lake, and an apartment in town. My sense was that they were richer than we were, though probably not as rich as Granny. I thought often in these terms.

Mrs. Coe was tall and very pretty, with light, curly hair that bobbed when she laughed. She moved in quick, long strides that I liked to watch. Her smile, I thought, stayed on her face longer than the others', and seemed more real. When she talked to me—we talked every time they came over, though usually not for long—it was not in the loud, public tones of the others, and not only to say how tall or handsome I would be, or to ask what I was doing in school.

She let me teach her pig Latin; we talked about the Brinks robbery and about the Yankees and Giants. She asked me once why I put things in my ears.

"What do you think of when you do it?" she said. We were sitting on the couch in our living room in New York. They had been the first guests to arrive; my parents and Mr. Coe were nowhere in sight.

"Nothing," I said.

"Not of the money it's costing your father, or the damage you could do to your ears?"

"No," I said. "I think of those things after."

"Well, will you do me a favor? Will you think of *me* next time?"

I said that I would try.

Then she opened her purse and took out the fattest package of jelly beans I had ever seen. There must have been five hundred, every color of the rainbow.

"I'll tell you what. You take out a handful of these every morning when you get dressed, and you put them in your pocket. Then, every time you think of sticking something in your ear, you know what you do?"

"I eat one."

"You eat one. You put a jelly bean in your mouth instead of some piece of plastic in your ear. And then you think of me. You know why?"

"No."

"Because I'll be thinking of *you*. I'm a mind-reader, you know, so you better watch out."

And then she kissed me.

Mr. Coe was a short, powerful-looking man with a gentle face, thick, bushy eyebrows, and an easy way of walking that reminded me a little of my father. He wasn't as much of a talker as his wife. We played games instead—card games, geography games, a game with dollar bills that involved the matching of serial numbers.

This one was my favorite. He called it "Golf." Each digit of the serial number was a "hole"; there were eight holes on every bill. To win, your digits had to be lower than your opponent's. When this happened, you won his bill and the game started again, each time with two new dollars. Mr. Coe, of course, provided the bills—he always came with plenty—replenishing mine whenever they ran out.

On average, I won three dollars. Once, though, as the grown-ups described it, I had a "hot bill"—ones and twos in most of the spots—and won ten in a row. My mother, who normally paid little heed to our games, arrived from nowhere to protest.

"That's too much, Walt. He'll think they grow on trees."

"Fair's fair, Ellie," Mr. Coe told her. "You can't change the rules in the middle of the game and expect him to ever trust you again."

My father agreed. "The money's his. Don't be such a prig." It was one of his five or six favorite terms.

But my mother, in a rare display of moral resolve, refused to be bullied.

"It's too much, it's too much," she kept saying. "Where do you draw the line?"

In the end, I was allowed to keep half of my winnings. It was called a "compromise," but I went to bed feeling robbed.

Other than this, though, I can't recall a single dissonant moment, at Massey Lake or in New York, on any night when there were guests. The camaraderie bordered on frenzy. When my father told a Jew joke, no one ever didn't roar. When the subject turned to the bedroom, the mischief and complicity were as thick as a school yard's.

And the lap-sitting—the dears and darlings, the quick, impulsive hugs, the cheek rubbings to compare beard stubble—subsumed it all, as the device of poker is subsumed when the only real object is to strip.

There was sex in the air. That would be one way of saying it. But the way I knew covered it just as well, and more on my terms. Everybody just *liked* everybody.

Fifteen

I don't remember when I first learned about my mother's headaches. I can't recall ever not knowing. They were as much a theme of our lives at home as the weekend parties, the nanny changes, or my father's bulldog rages. We adjusted to them. We learned not to be alarmed.

"Your mother has a headache."

It was a statement of the order of things—of the weather almost—like a reminder to wear galoshes. We reacted by rote: spoke in whispers in the hall, tiptoed past their bedroom, gave up all thought of seeing her face. It was as though she'd died temporarily.

She never came out of her room on her headache days. Meals were sent in and trays removed, often with the food still on them. She would occasionally ring for tea or juice. Bea and my father were the only ones who saw her. The silence, as pervasive as ever, was underscored now by need.

It would go on like this for a day or two, sometimes—rarely—

as long as a week. Then one afternoon we would come back from school or the park, and there she would be—in a dress or suit, on the couch or at her desk, hair combed, beauty spot in place, smiling her thin little after-headache smile. And we would know that the weather had cleared.

The headaches, which had been intermittent for years—since her teens or early twenties—had hit a new peak in the summer and fall of 1948. My sister had just been born. My father, nineteen years after the birth of his first son, finally had his little girl.

He was euphoric—bought cigars and Champagne for the doormen, carried her around on his hip on party nights ("Have you ever seen such gorgeous *feet?*") hours after she'd passed out, called her "Princess" and "Nicely-Nicely," and mooned through the months like a first-time father. He was forty-four, and possibly—for a time, at least—as nearly contented as he'd been in his life.

My mother, meanwhile, delivered at last from the failure of her firstborn child, in the afterglow of her daughter's birth—"the only good thing" to come of a thirteen-year marriage, her husband would say later—lay in the dark in eyeshades for most of four months, popped Seconal, and moaned at the ceiling.

The headaches eased that November, then began again in January, the week my father left for Albany. He would be gone—as he was now every year, "making laws"—weekdays through the middle of March.

My mother dreaded these months. Her days, as vacant and useless as ever, were followed now by nights that stretched endlessly, pointlessly, toward a sleep that rarely came before dawn.

She took little comfort in her children. We were reminders, at these times, of the emptiness she had married, the youth and boundlessness she had first wasted, then traded away. She missed the nights, nearly ten years behind her now, when sleep had been traded for gayer things. She felt old now, and unwanted. Her tummy had grown loose. She was thirty-four—bored, lonely, frightened, sick, and in pain.

It was in the winter of 1948–49 that she began drinking heavily alone. At first, as she would tell it later, only to dull the headaches. Then to compress the passing of time. By March, when my father returned, it was day and night. She couldn't leave the house without a drink.

When the pain—or depression or sleeplessness—was at its worst, she mixed whiskey with Seconal. Her appetite departed, she slept past noon. In late spring of 1949, she was diagnosed anemic. She had a blood transfusion, cut back on the pills, and forced herself to eat breakfast. Her weight flattened at a hundred and nine.

In June of that year, two weeks before my fifth birthday, my parents sailed for Europe. My father spoke of a "new beginning." They would eat more, drink less, tour the south of France, lie all day on the beach at St. Tropez, buy oblivion from the rigors of Albany, Wall Street, chicken-poxed children, and the carping nannies who tended them.

All this they did. They were gone two months, until the third week of August. The trip, recorded over four pages in my mother's album (but unreferenced in the suitcase), was a far cry from the inn-hopping bike odyssey she had shared with Bobby thirteen summers before. They drove south from Paris in a chauffeured gray sedan, stopping en route to take the baths at Divonne on the shore of Lake Geneva. From there they followed the Rhône as far south as Avignon, then drove east to Digne in Provence, where they spent a morning at Notre Dame and a day and night at a mineral-bath spa.

This left three weeks for the Riviera: Nice, Cannes, Monte Carlo, St. Tropez. My father played baccarat every night with a middle-aged French playboy; my mother swam and slept and sunned, and took day trips on the Mediterranean in boats chartered from village fishermen.

They arrived home two weeks before Labor Day and left the next morning for Massey Lake. My sister and I had been there since June, with Nanny and our summer cook, a gentle-natured black woman named Birdy whose specialty was a "shepherd's pie" that included every leftover from the week just past.

I remember the first weekend they were there. They dressed me, for a neighbor's costume party, in snorkle, goggles, galoshes, and bathing suit, put an oversize hat on my head and a lit flashlight in my hand, then hung a sign around my neck identifying me as the "Danforth Chemical Works," the Pittsburgh-based firm owned by a Massey Lake family.

I won first prize, and the riotous acclamation of all in attendance. I hadn't a clue what all the fuss was about—I had never heard of Danforth Chemicals, and probably couldn't read the sign in any case—but was delighted by my parents' hilarity, and by the magnum of Champagne I'd won, which I gulped from my father's glass until I got so dizzy and silly I had to be put to bed.

My half brothers, one sixteen, the other twenty, were with us that weekend. There is a picture of the three of us, taken in the garden in back of our camp, the afternoon of the costume party. I am standing between them, already in the galoshes and bathing suit I would wear that night, the top of my head reaching barely to Jimmy's waist. There is a hand on each of my shoulders. All three brothers are smiling.

I remember that picture—my mother took it, with my father directing from the porch—and the pride and bliss that went into my smile. All summer long, I had passed my evenings, and some of my days, in the company of a nanny I despised, a cook I barely knew, and a year-old sister who knew only how to slobber and cry. And now, miraculously, we were a family again. My brothers swung me from their shoulders with the strength of gods, my parents were in a jolly mood, and I was at the center of it all.

My mother must have felt some of the same sublimity. She filled two album pages with shots of that weekend.

But that was the end of it—our last, best hour as a family. Within a month of our return to the city, and the start of my kindergarten year, the headaches had returned. They were more monstrous now than ever. And other things, new things, came with them.

In the late winter of 1949–50, with my father again in Albany, my mother became agoraphobic. Crowds terrified her; she developed an obsession with public dining rooms. By the time he came home in March, she was too frightened, headache or not, to leave the apartment alone. Seconal and whiskey were her only relief. She continued to mix them, and continued to eat like a bird.

I don't know when the beatings began. Or *had* begun. It would be more than a year before she would tell of them, but they must have been happening by now. It would have taken more than words to increase the terror she had of him—and by now, of the world in general. We cringed together when he raised his voice.

I never saw him hit her. But I saw him, once, do worse. It was on one of our early-June car trips to Massey Lake. I don't remember what year, but my sister was still very small—and they had gone to Europe the summer she was one—so it was probably 1950. Eleanor was two, I was nearly six.

We were on a two-lane road, somewhere near Schenectady or Canajoharie in central New York. It was late afternoon, I think; the sun was still high. Eleanor and I were sitting in the back—with Nanny, I suppose, though I don't recall her at all. My parents were in front, screaming. My mother this time was fighting back.

The screams grew louder. I was pretending to read or color, my sister was crying. My father, it seemed, drove faster the louder he yelled. It was like riding in a bomb.

He hit the brakes, with what must have been most of his force. The car lurched, shimmied, then veered to the right. I remember the whine of tires, the sound of gravel underneath, and finally the dust that enveloped us.

We were on the shoulder, stopped, the front end angled toward the trees. For a second or two, there was no sound at all. Then my father reached across the seat—with deliberation, not violently—and opened the door on my mother's side. With his foot, or perhaps both of them, he pushed her out. I don't remember if she resisted. The last I saw of her, through the back window, she was sitting in the gravel, shrieking, getting smaller, as my father drove away.

I lost her around the first bend, and didn't see her again until—a day later, or two, or a week, I have no sense of the time that passed—she arrived at camp. I don't know where she'd been or with whom, how she got to us or why she came back (there is so much I don't know, and never will). I cared only that she had come home.

Sixteen

In the spring of 1951, following a siege of depression and migraine headaches so crippling she was paralyzed in her room for a week at one point, my mother was admitted to the Silver Hill Institute in New Canaan, Connecticut. The cost, for an "inexpensive room," was a thousand dollars a month.

"Mrs. Douglas is the daughter-in-law of Archibald Douglas, former chairman of the Memorial Hospital board. The Douglas family is socially prominent in NY, and well-to-do," wrote the referring gynecologist, who had urged that she go. It was his only comment, and stands alone on an otherwise nearly blank form titled "Prospective Patient."

She was admitted the afternoon of April 17, my sister's third birthday.

"She is a strikingly beautiful brunette woman, handsomely dressed, speaking in a deep, throaty voice," the admitting doctor wrote following a brief initial visit. "She went ahead to tell me that she had fears . . . gets panicky in a crowd, heart beats fast, she begins to sweat. She has been taking Seconal each evening for sleep, awakes in the morning depressed, hates to face the day."

A "Patient Profile" summarized the mileposts of her life:

She has been raised pretty much by governesses. . . . At 18, came out in NY, had a heavy social life, went to Bermuda in the springs, to Nantucket in the summers. She was married at 25, has lived in New York since. . . . Has done nurse's aid work, worked in a dress shop, dabbled in the decorating business. But now she has no interest in anything. Everything bores her. . . .

And her marriage:

She is the wife of a politician and [broker] ten years her senior who has two sons of his own. Husband said not to be able to control temper, possibly to need help from a nervous point of view. She has been sick for an indeterminate length of time—anxiety attacks, phobias, fatigue, dizziness, difficulty in concentrating, and migraine headaches. . . . Basically, I believe the husband situation to be the most important.

Her "average day" was described as follows—charitably, from what I knew of it:

Wakes at 7:30, lies in bed until 10:00, has orange juice and coffee in her room, makes a few phone calls, gets out of her room about noon, has two old fashioneds. Then maybe goes out to lunch, does a little shopping, comes back to the house, does a little telephoning, more cocktails, dinner at 7:45. Sits around home doing nothing in the evening.

"She seems to see herself as a battered butterfly, her husband as a Buddha or conceited dandy," a psychologist wrote in interpreting her test results. "She seems confused about her sexual role. . . ."

Her life, for the first time since her Farmington days, took on a matrix of order. Breakfast at eight, followed by a "tepid bath," an hour of shop, a forty-five-minute walk, an hour before lunch for "reading or writing." For ninety minutes each day she rested in bed—"doing nothing" was the prescription—and for thirty minutes she "studied." Tea was served daily at five-fifteen, dinner at seven. From eight to nine-thirty, she was "with people," after which she returned to her room, drank a cup of hot Ovaltine, and readied herself for bed. Lights-out was at ten, eleven on weekends.

She thrived. Within a week she had found her rhythm, seemed less depressed in her sessions, and was inquiring about paddle tennis. By the end of week two, she had gained three pounds, her sedative dose had been cut by a third, and she was sleeping through the night. She built a two-drawer pine desk for me during her hours at shop, stained it mahogany, and fitted it with brass handles. She hadn't shown such energy in years.

Still, she lacked courage. She had always lacked courage. She gilded the truth in protective evasions that offered less than they withheld. For every cloud, there was a silver lining:

> She says her husband is highly nervous, irritable, intolerant, he occasionally makes her sick. He is letting himself slip, he is lazy, he is bitter . . . but with all this, she claims to have a relatively happy marriage. They are in love, they have been faithful. . . . The sex is satisfactory, and there is enough of it (one should not take this as a truth without investigating with the husband). . . .
>
> He has a terrible temper. He has hit her, and said that she had better not allow him to get so mad he might kill her. But that was years ago. . . . He is very able, he has a good mind

(which she says he is not using), has a good sense of humor, he is well-liked. . . .

She promised Dr. ———— [the referring doctor] that she would tell me the entire story. This makes me think, since she emphasized it . . . that probably she didn't tell me the entire story. . . .

She was there nearly a month before her first furlough. On May 11, she left with my father for what was to be a week of spring fishing at Massey Lake. Her weight had flattened at a hundred and thirteen. She was sleeping well, had reported only one headache, and was said by her doctors to be gaining in resolve.

I remember that week. Vividly. It was the week another nanny got fired. This one, without a doubt, deserved it.

I don't remember her name, only that she had dark hair, a pinched mouth, and a voice as gravelly as a witch's. I loathed her—more, probably, than any nanny I'd had. She was a sadist. She spanked me with a hairbrush on my naked bottom until it hurt too much to cry, washed my mouth out with soap for telling her how much I hated her—" 'Hate' is the *devil's* word"—and read to me every night, interminably, from the Old Testament prophets ("I will turn your feasts into mourning, and your songs into lamentation; and I will bring up sackcloth upon all loins, and baldness upon every head"). When she was finished, we sang "Jesus Loves Me" together—holding hands—and I had to bless everyone I knew, beginning with her, in a prayer that got longer every night. If I missed anyone, she made me start again.

Every Sunday, rain or shine, we took the same walk: up the pedestrian path of the East River Drive from Sixty-first to Seventy-ninth Street, then back, Eleanor in a stroller, me on foot, grousing every step of the way. I was allowed to bring no toys, nor to lag behind nor run ahead. Every four or five blocks, at junctures determined at Nanny's whim, we would stop to admire some new wonder: a passing coal freighter, a tugboat, the way the sun came off the water. It was an endless, pointless, tedious promenade. I dreaded it all week.

But this Sunday was worse. I had a stomachache that grew sharper the farther we walked. I told Nanny. She told me the exercise would do me good. We reached Seventy-ninth Street and turned back. The pain was making it hard to walk; I felt sick now. Finally, somewhere about midway back, I vomited on the grass behind the benches that overlooked the river. I felt better instantly, though not for long.

We got home around five. The apartment was empty. Sundays were Bea's days off. She was still living, at the time, in Brooklyn with her husband; it would be another year before he would die and she would move into the vacant little room off our pantry. And even then she would be gone most Sundays. I hated Sunday nights.

I went to bed, wanting no supper. Nanny, unwavering in her view that constipation was at the root of every malady, fed me two tablespoons of Milk of Magnesia and left to put my sister to bed.

The pain was unbearable now. The worst I'd ever known. But the fear was worse. I was sure I was dying—and there was no help to be had. Only a witch and a baby to witness my end. I cried, then screamed, then screamed louder.

Nanny arrived with her Bible. She began reading. She read through my screams—serene, beatific, the true believer—as though they and I did not exist. Only God existed, speaking his Word through the mouths of the prophets, the damnation of Jehovah on the children of Israel.

I vomited on her Bible. I hadn't meant to. It was out of my mouth before I could know it was coming, covered the bib and sleeves of her white dress, and the pages of Amos or Jonah, in a frothy green mess that dripped onto her lap and shoes.

She turned white. She stared at me, then at the defiled Bible in her lap, as though at a ghost—or the devil himself. Then she rose from her chair by my bed, issued one constricted little gurgle of a cry, and proceeded to pummel me aimlessly on the face and head. I hardly felt the blows for the pain in my stomach, and my terror that even one of them would land there. None did. She ran from the room. I never saw her again.

The next thing I remember is the face of Dr. Anderson, looking down at me from what seemed like the top of a mountain. (Nanny, I suppose, must have finally sent for him, though I never knew for sure.) He was a grave, kindly man with thick white hair and meaty hands. I'd visited his office twice a year for as long as I could remember.

I was a very sick young man, he said, but I would be better soon. I had been brave; he was proud of me.

We drove to the hospital in his car, with me under a blanket in the backseat. He made a game of running the red lights—"Don't you ever try this when you grow up"—and never stopped talking the whole way there. I asked him if I was going to die. He told me no, of course not, and laughed at my silliness. But I could tell by the way he was driving that he wasn't so sure.

My appendix burst in the elevator on the way to the operating room. I don't remember this happening (I may have already been knocked out), but Dr. Anderson told me later, and showed me the appendix, a pint-sized collapsed squid, in a Mason jar filled with purple liquid that he brought to my room the next day. He told me again how brave I'd been, said that we'd had "a close call there for a while," and added that he hoped I liked vanilla milkshakes because I'd be drinking a lot of them for a while. (I drank almost nothing else for a month or more, and haven't even smelled one since.)

My mother was there when I woke up. Or at some point when I woke up, from surgery or from sleep. My father too.

They'd brought me presents. They were kind to me, especially her. She sat on my bed for what may have been an hour but seemed like only minutes, playing some game I can't remember—it may have been Chutes and Ladders. She told me several times how much she'd missed me—it had been a month—how proud she was of me, and how sorry for what "that awful woman" had put me through.

Then she kissed me, my father mussed my hair, and they were gone. She went back into the hospital—back "to Europe"—three days later. I wouldn't see her again for five weeks.

Her doctor's notes the Friday after my operation, summarizing the high points of her week away, include a string of references to the details of her headaches, her energy level, her husband's moods, the nature and amount of her drinking. A single four-word mention—"her boy got appendicitis"—is probably the best gauge to the emphasis she placed on the miscarriage of negligence that could have cost her her son.

All in all, her doctor concluded after seeing her that Friday, her week "didn't go that badly."

I think she loved her children—judging by the suitcase, we may have been *all* she loved those last few years. It was the sort of affection, though, that you might have for a favorite collie.

We were small, cute, endearing objects, sources of pride and entertainment, and—in my sister's case at least—of a common bond with an otherwise heedless husband. We were paraded out at the proper times to be petted, rewarded, or admired, then returned to the care of our keeper when the novelty had worn thin or our physical needs demanded attention.

Occasionally, for both parents, we were antidotes to loneliness or distractions from misery. Rarely, as in the case of my appendix, we were the source of a fleeting guilt. Except financially, we were not a responsibility. And even that was reluctant.

But saddest of all: They were no worse failures, as parents, than half of the parents they knew.

Soldierly nannies as surrogate mothers, six-year-old children as pets, a peck on the cheek at bedtime as the regimen-intimacy of a society mother with gayer things on her mind—you could field an army of childhood survivors, from a hundred Sutton Places, who could fill whole albums with hallmarks like these.

We were the children of privilege. Our privilege was its own reward.

Seventeen

Within days of my mother's return to Silver Hill, my father met—for the first time—with her doctor.

The impressions he left were not ambiguous. In the space of ninety minutes, by simply being himself, he managed to redefine both the prognosis and the course of treatment. The first dimmed markedly. The second, for a time, was derailed:

> As far as I'm concerned, he is the cause of Mrs. Douglas's illness. I asked him about her. He says she definitely has no drinking problem, that it's secondary to her nervousness. . . . He has no idea what has caused [her fears]. He says they get along fine except when they're fighting . . . that there is nothing wrong with him [except] a lack of purpose. . . .
>
> He is about as intolerant a person as I have ever run into. . . . Desperately prejudiced, very rigid and narrow-minded, a violent FDR hater, violent Jew hater, rabid in his hatred of England. Speaks of how Mrs. Douglas "came home

and started handing me this horse crap" that we are teaching here at Silver Hill. . . . All in all, I would say that anyone who had to live with Mr. Douglas would be nervous.

To me the situation looks practically hopeless. Here is this sort of sweet, dependent girl keeping up this front of poise and sophistication, living with a husband who I would guess is about as close to impossible as anyone [could be]. I don't really see what we are going to do. . . .

It was a new ballgame now. Reading today through the notes that followed that meeting with my father, you can almost see the doctors regrouping.

By the end of May, a second doctor had been brought into the case; there would eventually be a third. The tone of their notes grew blunter and more urgent ("This is a sick girl," "Keep her as long as possible"). My mother's phone calls were screened, there were more tests—IQ, Rorschach, TAT—the theme of her sessions veered sharply, from the past to the present tense.

The goal, for the time being, was maintenance. They redoubled their efforts to regulate her life:

She is not satisfied being a wife and a mother. And indeed, she has very few wifely-motherly duties to contend with, [having] a nurse and a maid and so forth. . . . If we could supply her with a purpose, if we could teach her to lead a balanced life, and if we could settle her alcohol problem for her, I think we will have accomplished a great deal.

Pills were the great equalizer. There was a pill—or "elixir"—for every mood, every ailment, every time of day. Five grains of Medinal—later replaced by chloral hydrate—to help her sleep; a Dexamyl tab at eight A.M., a second at eleven, to get her through the mornings. A half-grain of sodium Amytal at six P.M. to keep the depressions at bay. Migraines were met with Cafergot, later Gynergin; when she swung too high, there was phenobarbital to bring her down.

And her own remedies, a private stock: Seconal and a "pink medicine" she swore by as a last resort against insomnia. She became, over time, the product of her pills.

There is a lot to come out of her," her doctor had written in early May. "She has more to tell us, I feel sure."

By degrees, numbed by pills and reassured daily by the care and patience of her doctors, she began to shed her armor. She spoke— guardedly—of the details of her husband's drinking ("all day, all night, three drinks before lunch so he can relax to play golf"), his abuse of me, the fear he struck in her, her sacrifices, bitterness, obsessive fears, and confused sexuality: "She flirts, has to keep a tight rein on herself."

She showed her colors. "I am such a stupid person," she told her doctor at one point. "I feel so inadequate." And a week later: "Archie says I am no good. . . . I hate myself."

It had come to this. Everybody *hated* everybody, starting with themselves. Indolence, boredom, self-pity, all-day drinking, derision, and abuse. And at the end of the chain, for the more fragile of the two—the "butterfly" to her "Buddha"—a despair so thick and choking even her doctors could only wring their hands.

"I feel reasonably sure she is going to look back on this experience as a failure," one of them wrote in early June. "And so is her husband."

On the weekend of June 16, 1951, my father drove down from Massey Lake to New Haven for his twenty-fifth Yale reunion. Four days later he drove to New Canaan, as planned, to pick up his wife. She was discharged that afternoon, June 20, with the reluctant blessing of her doctors:

I think the prognosis must be extremely guarded. I have told her that we would want to hear from her every two weeks, either in person or by letter. . . . I am giving her a simple program with definite recommendations—regular hours of retiring and arising, exercise each day, an hour's reading. Urged no cocktails in the middle of the day. . . .

Her discharge papers noted a diagnosis of "depression in a cyclothymic individual faced with a difficult marital situation." The results of treatment, it said, "remain to be seen." The prognosis was given as "50–50."

I was late that summer leaving for Massey Lake. I don't remember why. Nanny and my sister had gone up ahead of me, probably with my father, sometime around June first.

By the second weekend of June, a week before my mother's discharge, I was still at home—with Bea or some short-term nanny, or both—or I may have been in Connecticut at my aunt and uncle's. I was sent there often when things were at loose ends.

My mother came home for a visit that weekend. I remember that she seemed quiet and tired and a little sad sometimes, but not nearly as bad as I'd seen her. She had no headaches that I could tell. She made time for me.

We sat together for a while in the dining room and talked about something—Massey Lake probably, and our plans for the summer—it wouldn't have mattered what. It was the first and last time in my life I ever had her to myself for longer than an afternoon.

She may have told me that weekend that she was coming home soon for good, if she knew it yet herself. But I don't remember that. She said that she had missed me and asked, as she nearly always did, if I had missed her too. I said that I had. We didn't talk—we never talked—about where she'd been. I don't remember when I first guessed that it wasn't Europe, or if I ever did.

She helped me pack—shorts, bathing suits, sneakers, a laundry bag full of my favorite toys and books. Then, in the early evening of her second or third day home, we took a taxi together in the rain to Grand Central.

I was not yet seven: about to ride a train through the night by myself, in a tiny raised cocoon of wool and fresh linen with its own private window, which you could climb up into and zip closed. It was the first great adventure of my life.

I remember every sight and sound, every smell. The grimy gray platform with its dull, faraway lights; the long, dying wheeze of the engines in their bays, the crush of people and luggage; the fat, red-faced conductors in their dark blue caps and jackets who hollered life-and-death gibberish to each other between cars. I was in awe.

I can't imagine, knowing what I know today, how my mother managed it. A crowded street corner gave her sweats; Grand Central Terminal at the tail end of rush hour must have been a kind of hell.

But I noticed nothing. We found my berth, an upper in mid-train facing away from the platform. And Booker: shorter than my mother and blacker than Bea, with a slate-bald head, a crisp white linen jacket that stopped at the waist, and a smile he seemed to have been born with. Booker, my mother said, would take care of me.

Booker said the same, grinned his big grin, and tugged on one of my ears: "The way I'm gonna be tuggin' on your toe—*that* one there—'bout fifteen minutes to four in the mornin'. You ever been up four in the mornin', young fella?"

I liked Booker, though I never saw his face again—except fleetingly at four in the morning—after my mother left the train. I don't know if I slept at all that night. Through four hundred miles of darkness, my little window informed me: that trains running next to highways, once their speed picks up, are faster than most cars; that when a train goes by the other way, the heads in its windows are a blur of small stumps; that the lights in stations late at night shine down onto signs there is no one there to read. I was the only one alive in the world, I thought: wide awake, maybe still dressed, when Booker yanked my toe.

An old woman in a beat-up brown station wagon she called a taxi met me at the station in St. Regis Falls. It was cold and still dark. The woman had long gray whiskers growing out of her chin, and looked like she might die at any moment. She made me sit in front with her—I'd never been in the front seat of a taxi—but hardly talked at all, for which I was thankful.

It was red in the distance by the time she dropped me off. No one was awake. I went down to the lake with my fishing rod, but it was too shallow off our dock to sink a worm, so I went after tadpoles in the reeds with a tennis-ball can until Nanny came down and said it was time for breakfast.

The summer of '51 was the beginning of the end for my mother. As for me, it was the best summer of my life. I learned to do the crawl that June, and was allowed for the first time—as a birthday present—to take a boat out alone. I took tennis lessons, and by Labor Day could serve overhead and keep the ball in play. It would be three or four more years before I learned to cast a fly, but it was that summer that I caught—trolling, on a worm—the largest trout I would catch for ten more years to come. I was seven now, a veteran of first grade, and Nanny's tether had never been so long or so loose.

I have almost no memories of my parents that I can connect, with any certainty, to that summer. My father was with me in the boat when I caught my big trout; and I remember standing under a tree on the Watchee River, a week or two later, watching him land one almost as big—it had hit his fly in precisely the patch of water he'd predicted.

Other than this, though, and some snippets that could as easily belong to any other summer, my parents don't enter in. It was a high-flying, magical three months—the best I'd ever had—but it seems in my mind to have happened without them.

My mother arrived at camp more than two weeks after me, three days before my seventh birthday. She had come for the summer. She lasted twelve days.

I don't know what happened to break her. I can't help but feel, though, that it was more than she let on:

"Ten days ago, suddenly out of the blue at the time of her menstrual period, came another depression," her doctor reported the morning she was readmitted to Silver Hill. "A downhill run 'so bad I wanted to die.'

"She has been depressed, panicky, has lost 4–5 pounds. . . . She has had to drink to get things done. . . . She has thought of suicide. Says she wouldn't do it, but that definitely she wouldn't mind dying."

The doctors were at a loss. "Why is Mrs. Douglas on the defensive at times?" one of them puzzled nakedly in his notes in mid-July. "How did she get this way? There is quite a preoccupation with sex. [I need] to find out the nature of that. . . . She puts up a good front."

The front wasn't budging. Her husband had been "wonderful," she said, during their twelve days together at Massey Lake. There had been "little in the environment that would have caused her slide."

Her doctors, with a reluctance you can almost touch as you read their notes, played the cards she dealt them. Her depressions, they concurred, were "endogenous"—meaning basically that they caused themselves. Their prescription, which my mother seemed almost relieved to comply with, was electroshock therapy.

She was checked into the Neurological Institute in Manhattan on the morning of July 16, six days after her flight from Massey Lake. Early that afternoon, she had her first shock treatment. Over the course of the next nine days, she would have five more.

She had been scheduled for seven. With five behind her, she remained on course: "Only minimal evidence of memory disturbance. Her mood level is good," the hospital noted the afternoon of July 24.

She had her sixth treatment the following morning, a Wednesday. My father, in New York for the week, saw her within hours of it. He called her doctor at home that night:

"He said Mrs. Douglas was upset, that she had had a profound memory disturbance and confusion with the treatment, also an insulin reaction with a lot of perspiration in the morning. She thought she had had too many treatments, wanted to come home."

She was transferred back to Silver Hill the afternoon of July 26. She was shaky. Her memory was "a little disturbed." She was housed in special quarters, given a round-the-clock nurse. Her pride had suffered badly.

"She is mad—mad that we gave her the treatments, mad that she has a nurse, that she is at the River House, that we did this to her mind. . . . She feels tired, has pimples on her face, a sty in her eye, a boil on her mouth. . . . She acts a little distracted. I don't think she concentrates very well yet."

I try to picture her like that. Only tintypes come to mind: Lilith, Anne Sexton, Edie Sedgwick. A young woman I once knew, in my own battle for sanity—but I was nineteen, not thirty-six, and my demons were behind me—with the IQ of an Einstein, a need for love so naked you had to look away, and self-inflicted cigarette burns covering her eyelids and wrists.

She was losing her self, and must have known it. Her power was gone, her beauty was going. She had pimples and boils. Her hus-

band hated her, her friends had forgotten her, she had failed—
if she'd ever tried—as a mother and wife. She couldn't think
straight. Pills and liquor were her only revenge, and they savaged
no one but herself.

There wasn't a dream she'd ever owned that had a chance at
fulfillment. The best she could do was survive. And survival was
worse—a tunnel without an end.

Eighteen

They had been married eleven years and three months when my mother fled from Massey Lake, like a panicked deer, that July of '51. Seventy-one pages of photos, spanning most of two albums, mark her record of those years.

But as the times had grown more joyless, the record had grown thin: Of the eight pages she'd filled since their Riviera resort binge of two Augusts before, nearly all were of her children. And all of these were of summers at Massey Lake.

For years now, there had been little to hold fast to but the summers. And she hadn't missed one.

I toddled and giggled in '46; discovered water, in a bright orange life jacket (the first year of color Kodaks) in July of '47. In '48 my sister, bald and diapered at three months, got top billing with a page of photos, though I managed a walk-on with my father in the bow of a boat. I was the Danforth Chemical Works, a doting big brother, and a thoughtful young man in a beached rubber raft, all in the summer of '49. In '50 I caught my first fish ("14 inches"), Eleanor sat on my lap on our dock and sucked on a snorkle. Even Nanny took a bow.

And then it stopped. Like a wound-down toy. Dead in the middle of a left–right spread—"Camp '50"—with the summer barely half over and Eleanor and I huddled together on that dock, two and six, with three more summers still to give her, my mother put down her camera and quit. The right-hand page sits empty. It's as though there'd been a train wreck.

The album itself wasn't quite finished, though it probably should have been. The three pages that remain are a shoddy testament, even to what little was left of her life.

On the first two, originally a seven-photo spread of a deer-hunting weekend with the Coes in the autumn of 1950 ("Bag: 2 Buck, Take: 1 Case"), only a single picture survives: of my mother and Vivian Coe, sitting shoulder to shoulder at the base of a thick birch, neither one smiling, a bottle in both their hands.

Of the six missing photos, only the mountings remain. I can't account for them. She must have destroyed them later, no doubt for a reason.

The final page—"New Year's '51"—records a party roughly two months later. Six couples are represented, including five that I knew. In one picture, my mother, her head thrown back, is entwined drunkenly with a tall, silver-haired man, the only one I don't remember.

In another—the last photo, of the page and of the album—my father and Vivian Coe are pressed together on a couch, both laughing wildly, her head tipped back into his, one arm draped around his shoulder.

The two pictures are end-to-end. She may have meant them as a final portrait. In any case, they are.

There's no telling when exactly my father and Mrs. Coe began their affair. My mother wouldn't tell of it until nearly the spring of '52, but that's no gauge to anything. By then, the Coes were only barely a couple, and the Douglases were so engulfed in liquor, pills, and hate that adultery was only one more brick on the pile.

It may have begun as early as the deer-hunting weekend or the New Year's Eve party, or even before. Or they may have been just preludes. But whenever it started, I assume I know when it took root to stay: in that feckless, fool's-paradise summer of my seventh year, while I was tearing between camps in our new guide boat like a teenager with his first car keys, and my mother was dodging the truth at Silver Hill or between shock treatments in New York.

My father was a bachelor most of those weeks. The Coes were next door. I don't know what happened between the three of them—if Walt Coe was accomplice or cuckold, if my father was dallying or playing for keeps. But I know what grew from that summer; I know what sprang from its roots. And if the end says anything about the beginning, they were planted deep.

My mother was with us at camp barely four weeks from June to September: the twelve days that ended in mid-July with her "out of the blue" seizure and flight, less than a week in early August, and twelve more days around Labor Day.

Each time was like the first. She arrived resonant and hopeful, fortified with good intentions—then retreated like a routed army, with half-packed bags on the first train that would take her, racked by headaches and terrors, days or weeks before she'd planned.

Whatever she saw, or thought she saw, or tried to be a part of, it bent her mind with the force of a waking nightmare.

"She woke up yesterday panicked, frightened, wondered if she was going crazy," her doctor reported on August 8, 1951, the day of her second unscheduled arrival at Silver Hill in less than four weeks. "I collected all the medicines she had with her. I don't consider her suicidal at present, but we will have to watch her carefully."

My father's summer—its daylight parts—continued undisturbed. He was at camp weekends, as he was every year, and for parts of some weeks. In mid-July, when my mother called and asked that he come to New York to be with her for her first shock treatment, he complained that it would require him to cut short a weekend (though he went in the end). So, while I can't say for sure how he passed his days that summer—my memories, or most of them, attach to no certain year—I have no reason to suppose they were much different from any other. Only freer.

In the mornings, he played golf. I don't remember his departures, only his returns—usually around my lunchtime or a little after, with Mr. Hubbard, Mr. Fitch, and sometimes some third man. They would sit together in the living room, always in high spirits, and drink and joke and compare scorecards.

The talk was always the same: doglegs, three-putt greens, two-dollar Nassaus, and all the other things that were part of that same strange language that belonged to golf. I didn't understand a word of it, but I liked to listen—to drink ginger ale in my chair by the window and to laugh when they laughed.

I was doing this one day when Mr. Fitch called me over. "How's your arithmetic?" he asked.

I said it was all right, then waited for my father to correct me. He didn't. I had the feeling I was about to be made a goat. It happened a lot; I was used to it. The worst part was, I never knew what exactly I had said or done that made them laugh.

"Probably better than mine," Mr. Fitch said. I replied, earnestly, that I was sure it wasn't.

"Well, let's just find out. Tell you what—you add up those numbers there, in those boxes under my name, and let's see what you get. If your total's the same as mine"—he had erased his total from the bottom of the card—"I'll give you this half-dollar. If I like it *better,* you get an even buck."

Everybody roared. I had no idea at what. I added the numbers, as carefully as I could, with paper and pencil, on my knees in front of the fireplace, then handed him the result. It must have been wrong.

He took one look, leaped out of his chair, pulled a dollar from his pocket, and shook it in my face. When I made no move to take it—I hadn't a clue if this was a joke, a game, or something more serious—he let it drop to the floor and began jumping and spinning around the room, waving his scorecard in front of his face as though it were on fire.

"I *knew* it! I *knew* it! Only thing wrong with my game's my goddamn addition! *Six under par!* Can you believe it? *Pay up,* boys! I told you the kid would bail me out!"

I never understood what the bet had been about, only that I had won money for the wrong side. I felt foolish and betrayed, and tried to give my dollar to my father to make up for the loss I had cost him. He only laughed, though, said that a bet was a bet, and told me to keep my winnings.

Other times he went fishing. This was more serious—more ritual than entertainment—involved greater preparation, and promised higher rewards.

The trips could range from two hours to three or four days, from an evening's bass-troll on Massey Lake to a twenty-mile canvass of the Watchee or Red Jacket rivers, casting for brookies and rainbow in the pools beneath the rapids and sleeping in lean-tos built into the rocks, in abandoned fire wardens' cabins, or in tents they took with them and pitched on high, dry ground near wherever they wanted to be fishing when they woke with the sun the next day.

I loved watching him prepare for these trips: oiling his reels, cutting his leaders, poring over what flies to use for the hatch or the cold spell he was always sure was coming. His hands moved like wands. His eyes squinted over the tiny eyelets with a fixedness I marveled at. He was master of his gear: a gentle, patient mastery that left him, at least for those few hours, at peace with his world.

I think I sensed this. I know that I knew, even then, that his preparations were more ceremony than necessity, that they offered him something that had little to do with the catching of trout.

The joy he took in them, and in fishing itself, came close to reverence. He seemed almost tender. And in that softness, for me, there was a safety I felt at no other time. When I want or need, today, to think good things of my father, I think of him casting a fly.

They left usually in late afternoon, stooped forward under heavy, open-topped wicker packs their maids had spent the morning preparing: steak, eggs, bacon, butter, cans of peas and peaches, jam, peanut butter, mustard and Worcestershire, clean shirts and trousers, bedrolls, underwear, socks and boots, a spare rod, a roll of toilet paper, bottles of whiskey and beer.

They were gone two days, or three, then returned: tired and stubble-faced, stinking of sweat and fish—they had always caught fish, sometimes only a dozen, sometimes a hundred or more—their packs almost weightless now, their strides slower and shorter than when they'd left.

There were always stories, and not only of trout. A mountain lion had neared their fire one night, a moose and its babies had crossed the river forty feet upstream; it had rained so hard the trail had washed out, a black bear had eaten their bacon; one of them had slipped in the rapids and nearly gone under, another had pulled him out. They had prevailed. They had been men.

They had their catch to show for it: rainbow and brookies, a few nearly as long as my arm. Half of those summer mornings we ate trout. And each of them too, I knew, carried its story. It wasn't hard to imagine the stories—I'd seen my father fish. By the summer I was seven, more times than I could count.

I'd watched him lay his fly, sometimes two or three times in an afternoon, at the precise center of a rise forty feet away in a gusting wind, then pull his line taut against a trout, sinking the barb, before I'd even seen the swirl. He never flinched or smiled when the fish hit, just drew his lips back ever so slightly and narrowed his eyes. The perfection made me shiver. There was no skill in the world I wanted so badly to master.

I can do it today—half as perfectly—though he never lived long enough to see me reach my best. I've loved trout fishing since the first summer he tried to teach it to me, the summer I was six. I've wondered often, though: how much of my love is for the sport itself—its simple drama, the rush I get, every time, at the sight of dark water—and how much is for the link it once gave me to a father who brought to it a ministry he couldn't manage for his son.

It doesn't matter. Fishing was his gift to me, and I treasure it. But I wonder nonetheless.

For my mother, the summer ended as it had begun. She was a creature of her habits now. And of her pills. She lurched between trauma and solace like a blinded fighter groping for the ropes.

On August 20, she was released from Silver Hill following a twelve-day stay, her third in as many months. As always, she seemed improved. But no new ground had been broken. The cause of her miseries, for whatever reasons, she was keeping to herself.

On August 24, a Friday, she arrived at Massey Lake. A fishing trip was planned, probably with the Coes, on the north fork of the

Watchee River. She was to return to New York with my father two weeks later, Sunday, September 9.

One more time, she spooked and fled. By September 5, she was back at Silver Hill: "run down, shaky, as bad as she has ever been." She was asked the causes of her flight. She offered nothing. The trip had been uneventful, she said.

Her doctors, having nothing to work with but her pain and her fear, treated what they had as radically as they knew how. She was transferred to the Neurological Institute. Over eleven days in mid-September, she was given six more shock treatments.

She went home the afternoon of September eighteenth—the same day we did. We arrived after dark with my father, another summer ended. She was probably there by the time we got in, but I doubt we saw her. Her memory loss, though "minimal," is not something she would have shared.

I don't know if her terrors were real, imagined, or something of both. I don't know what happened on that fishing trip. I don't know who or what she thought she was protecting—her pride, her marriage, her illusions—or if she even knew herself. I try to read past the sterile compassion of her doctors' notes, past the pictures she took and left untaken, and the thousand dim memories I have, and make some sense of her pain. Of her paralysis.

I can't. I've become a student of her life. I know the motives and instincts and terrors that drove her, I am older and wiser than she ever lived to be. But I do not understand.

There can *be* no understanding, I think, of the world she'd been reduced to. She was nothing in that world. A cipher, without purpose or worth. She *had* nothing—only her pain, her pills, and the distractions of the moment.

With my father, it was different. He lived somewhere beyond his own judgments, in a fashioned morality only a handful understood. He had his terrors too, and ran from them: cheated, lied, drank himself to an early death. But there was a symmetry to the world he invented—Republicans and Yale men, niggers and kikes, the masses in between—that made sense to him, that he would die, corruptedly, believing.

He was weak, coddled, misguided, and cruel. And dishonest to others. But never—entirely—to himself. He believed. His father and mother and Yale and Wall Street had helped him believe, had in some things believed with him: that the world would be a better place If —, that rank and destiny are interlocked, that when a deserving man falls short, the fault, nearly always, is with an undeserving world.

You can go to your grave almost peaceful believing all that— although, to his credit, I don't think he did.

But my mother. She believed in nothing. She believed in her waist size, her smile, and her debutante's tool kit. When they were gone—or moot—she was a dance without music. An abstraction. Condemned by definition to disuse.

Nineteen

Life went on, for all of us. I entered second grade in the fall of '51.

We had a new nanny, tolerable this time: German, short and pudgy—as outsized as all the rest—but with a heart I learned to trust, and a comic, swivel-hipped bustle that got her from pantry to bedroom so quickly my mother once joked that there were two of her.

She taught me the first two verses to "O, Tannenbaum"—an improvement on the prophets. I taught her "Jingle Bells." She got on famously with Bea, which counted for a lot in our house. My mother too. She was with us nearly two years—a record—and when she finally left I cried.

My mother was home that fall, and for most of the winter that followed. Life seemed to have smoothed. On our shopping trip to Best's that September (three days following her last shock treatment, perhaps less), she told me she was coming home to stay. She was tired, she said, from being away so much. She needed time to rest.

But once she was rested, on some sunny weekend day before the weather got cold, she would give Nanny the day off. We would "do the town" together—the zoo, a movie, FAO Schwarz. I should think about what I'd like it to be.

I don't know if I believed her. I probably did. But I seized the moment anyway: I'd missed almost all of my allowances, I said, while she'd been away. I had kept track. I offered a list.

We were in a taxi, on our way home. The seat between us was piled with shopping bags. She took three dollars from her purse and handed them across to me:

"Now, let's not talk about money anymore." She seemed suddenly very tired.

I felt her sadness. I had ruined something. We were quiet the rest of the way home. I gave Nanny the three dollars, that night, to return to her, but they came back again the next day.

We never did do the town together. Except for two more September pre-school trips to Best's, I don't think we ever went anywhere together again. But she tried. Everyone tried that fall.

She read to me: *Black Beauty,* on and off for two weeks or a month of bedtimes, the first and only book we ever shared. She said it had been read to her as a girl, by her mother, that it had been her favorite.

I loved *Black Beauty*—the loss and hope it swung between, the full-page period pictures of horses and men. About the readings themselves I remember very little—only that I came to count on them, that I cried once when Beauty was sold away to a cruel master, and that my mother's voice seemed very warm and sure.

It never occurred to me, until now, in opening the book for the first time in nearly forty years, that her reasons for choosing it—conscious or not—may have been darker than she said.

Black Beauty is a story—a parable, really—about courage and fate:

". . . A horse never knows who may buy him or who may drive him; it is all a chance for us, but still I say, do your best wherever it is, and keep up your good name."

Its accounts of oppression and futility—even in the lives of story-book horses—had to have struck a chord:

It was Ginger! But how changed! The beautifully arched and glossy neck was now straight and lank . . . the face, that was once so full of spirit and life, was now full of suffering. . . .

I said, "You used to stand up for yourself if you were ill-used."

"Ah," she said, "I did once, but it's no use; men are strongest, and if they are cruel and have no feeling, there is nothing that we can do, but just bear it, bear it on and on to the end. I wish the end was come, I wish I was dead. I have seen dead horses, and I am sure they do not suffer pain. . . ."

To have chosen *that* book. To have read aloud—sweetly, mother-like—those words. In the dregs of her life, as the only book her son would remember her by. Could she have known—could she *not* have known, if she'd thought about it, even once—that he would open its pages one day and hear her cry?

Michael Phillips lived upstairs from us. On the seventh floor, I think. We may have met on the elevator; I can't imagine how else. He didn't go to Buckley, or to any school I'd heard of; he didn't roller-skate in the park. Our parents barely knew one another.

However it happened, we became friends. And while there's no way of placing a value on friendships between second-graders, if Michael Phillips wasn't the best friend I'd ever had, he was certainly the most important—though it would be twenty years before I saw this.

Michael was a Catholic. A mackerel-snapper, the only one I knew. His family had no maid or nanny. There were dirty dishes in their kitchen sink; the chairs in their living room had grease stains on the arms. They ate off plates without patterns; their forks came out of kitchen drawers.

Michael's mother was pretty, but not the way mine was. She wore scruffy brown loafers; her face in the mornings looked tired. Her hair, which was dark and straight, fell down over her eyes in strands when she cooked or rinsed dishes—in a kitchen half the size of ours. She blew it sideways and went on rinsing. I wondered that she wore no combs or pearls.

Michael's father frightened me a little, but only until I learned to read him. Mr. Phillips was stern and strict, in a military fashion, and wasted few words. Michael called him "Sir." But he smiled as often as he frowned, and his praise was worth something.

He was short and powerful-looking, with curly gray hair cut close to his head. He and Michael played handball together in the park. I'd never known anyone before who played handball, or who called his father "Sir."

I began escaping there: between homework and supper, supper and bed. It was a simple matter—two flights up, two back, "in a whisk," as Nanny said. I was hardly missed.

My stays grew longer. I was asked for supper—meatloaf probably, and potatoes, peas or corn—at a dish-piled table with everyone telling of their days. I returned downstairs to the silence. The next day—or week—I was back. Then for the night, then a weekend. It became a second home.

My father, had he known, would have put a stop to it. A "stigma," he'd have said. But he paid no notice, in the best of times, to how I spent my days.

The Phillipses must have known this, or some of it. About my father, my mother's illness, the way things were with us. It was not a large building; their invitations were never returned. But if they knew, they gave no sign. There were no proddings, no judgments, no sympathies expressed.

They were kind, only that. They treated me as they treated their son. I walked my plate to the kitchen after dinner was finished, cleaned up after my messes, observed the rules of their home. In return, they let me feel a part of it. Wise people, with good hearts.

They *did* things with Michael. And therefore, after a time, with me. On weekend afternoons with Mrs. Phillips, we took the subway to the zoo, to Radio City, and once, I think, to a baseball game. Subways, Michael's mother explained to me, cost less than taxis, and there was more to see.

This was a hard lesson to digest—"Subway Sam," in our home, was a catchall for all the urchins and sloths of the world. But in time I came to see its truth. Black people, brown and yellow, strange old graybeards in tunics and hats—the rabbi, Mrs. Phillips said, is a "holy teacher"—dark women with handkerchiefs drawn across their faces like cowboy bandits. Santa Claus himself rode the subway.

And all of them close enough to touch. I learned more about the world in one afternoon of subway-gawking with Michael and his mother than in a year from the windows of cabs.

Mrs. Phillips must have marveled at the smallness of my world. She answered every question: What was it like to be Catholic? ("We believe in the same God as you.") Where do poor people sleep? Are blind beggars always faking? Do Negroes wear underpants?

She talked with me, we played games, she found my strengths:

"What rhymes with cafeteria?"

"Bacteria," I said.

"Bacteria—that's very, very good. Michael, do you know what bacteria is?"

Michael said he didn't.

"I'm not surprised. That's a big word for a seven-year-old. You know, Geoffrey, you're very good with words."

I hadn't known. But it was true, I was. And from that moment, in a subway car in the spring of my second-grade year, a new consciousness bloomed in my world. I would never let it go.

I don't remember how things ended with the Phillipses. They may have moved away before we did, or I may have just stopped going upstairs. I saw Michael years later, when we were both seniors at boarding school—the Jesuit school he attended was in the same town as the school I'd landed at after St. Paul's—but our friendship never really picked up.

I don't know how strong it had been in the first place. It was his family I'd gone to see: the *idea* of the four of us, the loud, sloppy dinners, Mrs. Phillips's careless laughter, the attentions they paid.

I suspect it may have worked both ways: The boy downstairs had troubled parents, his only company were nannies, they had a son the same age, maybe they could help. They would have thought that way. They were good, wise, religious people. Their charity began at home.

If that was their angle, or even part of it, they should know today, wherever they are—I've tried to trace them, but I never even knew Mr. Phillips's first name—that I left richer from their suppers, their subways widened my world. I am thankful. They did their work well.

It was the time of my ear-stuffings. Between these and my braces—which I would suffer with through fifth grade—I spent half my afternoons, it seemed, in doctors' chairs. And nearly as many weekend mornings on the couch in our living room, nodding mindlessly at my father's ravings about the "goddamn fortune" being "pissed away" on my ears and mouth.

Money was a big topic with him. Next to politics—to which it was often linked, in ways I barely understood—it was probably his biggest. To hear him tell it, we were in troubled straits. At least weekly, there were tirades: doctors' bills, tuition costs, clothes, nannies, hairdressers, the "thieves" in Albany and Washington.

Even my allowance. It was a quarter a week, though I almost never got it except when my mother was at home. Only once did I dare remind him. He took off his belt, let it dangle dangerously from his fist like a gunfighter fingering his Colt, and glared at me through the thinnest, coldest eyes he could muster. He didn't say a word. I dropped my gaze. He put the belt back on, as languidly as he'd removed it.

For my mother, the subject of money was off-limits in his presence. But she worried about it endlessly. Their finances were a disaster, she had told her doctor. They spent prodigally when times were flush; when the market sagged and my father's checks grew thin, there was sometimes not enough to cover Bea's check. And still she kept her silence. The alternative, she said, was a hundred times worse.

I don't know how bad things really were, but there may have been some basis to all this. My father's income, in an average year, was fifty thousand dollars. A lot of money at the time. But with a full-time maid and nanny, an apartment on Sutton Place, a Buckley tuition, a son each at Yale and St. Paul's, a trip a year to Sun Valley or the south of France, and a thousand dollars a month in psychiatrists' bills—never mind the braces and eraser bits—it's not hard to imagine that they may have been strapped.

Still, I doubt things ever got ultimate. His mother was a phone call away. And while I don't know how many advances he took on the inheritance he would never live to see, I'm certain there were some—just as I'm certain that every bill he couldn't cover without calling on Granny was another dent in his manhood, another hour of torment for his wife.

She is sliding up and down," her doctor wrote the third week of October. He was seeing her now weekly—Wednesdays—at his office in the city. They talked almost daily by phone.

The battle now was for maintenance. "Sane living" was the term they had coined. Their sessions revolved around issues of regimen:

more sleep, less booze, exercise, and "acceptance." My mother had enrolled at a ballet school on West Fifty-fourth Street—two dollars a class—though I don't know how often she went. The idea, it seems, was to take life a day at a time.

Whatever small progress she'd been making, it ended soundlessly, a puff of smoke that left no trace.

In mid-November, in what was becoming an annual event, my parents drove together to Massey Lake for a week of deer hunting. My mother phoned her doctor five days before they left. She needed more pills, she said.

He must have been puzzled; she'd cut her dose in half in the weeks just past. In any case, he complied. The prescription—Medinal and Dexamyl—was delivered to a pharmacy on Madison Avenue.

There is no record of that hunting trip, nor of who, if anyone, went with them. But it's probably safe to say they didn't go alone. They went nowhere alone anymore.

She saw her doctor on November 28, the Wednesday after their return. Something had happened. She wouldn't—or couldn't—say what. Only that they'd shot no deer. She was a wreck again: couldn't sleep, couldn't eat, she had the shakes. Her mind, she said, "goes all night long." But she didn't want to talk about it. She only wanted more pills.

The slide continued. By two Wednesdays later, she was shaking so badly she had to sit on her hands to keep them still. Her old fears were back. She was too afraid, she said, to leave the house alone. It was the last appointment she would keep.

Her doctor had despaired. "What is behind this neurosis?" he mulled in his notes, defeated, after their last session together. "I have never found out. It looks like I am never going to. . . ."

Whatever had happened that November week at Massey Lake, whatever old wounds it opened or new ones it begat, it cut through the flimsy bit of fabric still knitting their lives—the pretenses, the "sane living," the pathetic attempts at order—like a razor through gauze. From that week on until the end, twenty-two months later, they were as naked as plucked birds. They unraveled, both of them, together and apart, in an almost untrackable blur.

Nine days after my mother's last session with her doctor—four days before Christmas—Silver Hill got a call. It was from Fritz Hubbard, one of the weekend regulars. Things were out of hand, he said. Something had to be done. He didn't know how to reach my mother's doctor in the city; he didn't know where else to turn.

Of all my parents' men friends, I liked Fritz Hubbard the best. He was crazy—the kind of crazy kids love. He was a kid himself: painted mustard streaks on his face and did war dances in our living room, howled lovestruck moose calls out the window to pedestrians five floors below, went to a Yale hockey game once in a raccoon coat with nothing on underneath but red underpants and garters. He'd been a class behind my father at Yale, and his best friend ever since.

I knew him as Uncle Fritz. His life would be a ribbon of tragedies—some avoidable, some not—but he would survive them all with his craziness intact. Or so it always seemed to those of us looking on.

It would be Fritz Hubbard, twenty years later, who would toast my Uncle Jack as "the finest little brother Archie Douglas could have had."

He'd arrived at our apartment without notice, he told the doctor he spoke with, at one in the afternoon the Wednesday before Christmas. My parents had just gotten up.

They'd been out till seven in the morning. They didn't tell him where, or say if they'd been together or apart. They were a wreck, he said. My father, still half-drunk, was chasing his grapefruit with whiskey. He'd been sick, in bed most of the past week, "taking some kind of shots."

Uncle Fritz was worried. He ran in the same crowd they did, had a camp at Massey Lake, had known the Coes for years. He knew the score. But this was beyond what a friend could sit still for: Something had to be done.

Nothing was done. Nothing could be. My mother's sessions with her doctor had lapsed. My father was drunk half the time, absent the rest, his whereabouts unknown. It must have been a hellish Christmas. I have no memory of it at all.

My father left for Albany the day after New Year's. My mother retreated to her bedroom and her pills. For close to two weeks, from Mondays to Fridays, Bea was the only one to see her face.

On January 16, 1952, a Wednesday, she phoned her doctor in New York. He hadn't seen her in nearly five weeks. She needed more pills, she said. Would she have to leave home to get them?

Three bottles, a total of a hundred capsules—Dexamyl, Medinal, Cafergot—were delivered to our door the same day. They lasted nineteen days.

On February 5, she called Silver Hill. Life was unbearable, she said. She couldn't sleep, couldn't keep her food down, her pills had lost their power to blot out her days. Her New York doctor was on vacation, she had nowhere else to turn. What should she do? The hospital promised to get back to her.

There's no record of when or whether it did. But ten days later, February 15, my parents arrived together at Silver Hill. Both of them, finally, were too weary and beaten for disguises:

I first saw him. He looks terrible, smells of alcohol, looks tired, bloodshot eyes. . . . He is in Albany a lot now, has not seen much of her. He is under a lot of pressure ("It's an election year, doctor"). . . .

He is fed up. . . . She nags, he nags. Since SH, she has been impossible. We said she had a good IQ, now she thinks she is Einstein. "A woman should be taught she is dumb, treated accordingly."

He says he [feels] rotten, has hypertension, has lost ten pounds, is not sleeping. She does not sleep [either], does not eat. . . . She is depressed, jittery, can't get out of the house, is drinking for medicinal purposes. . . .

Then I saw her. . . . The past two weeks have been awful. Has all her old fears back, nausea, gagging, panics, not eating, hairdressers terrify her. . . .

They are talking of divorce. He drinks like a fish, starts in the morning. . . . Family and friends all think it incredible she stays with [him]. . . .

She told me also that Archie has a lady love, one of their best friends. . . .

He says to her: "For Christ's sake, go out and have an affair. . . ."

Less than two weeks later, on the Saturday of Washington's Birthday weekend, 1952, my mother was admitted—"depressed, gaggy, exhausted, full of fears and panics, smoking two packs a day"—for what would be her final stay at Silver Hill.

Fourteen years earlier, on the same Saturday in 1938, she had arrived at the Laurentide Inn in St. Agathe, a twenty-three-year-old Bonwit's model with moon dust in her eyes and a man on each arm. She had said good-bye to one of them that weekend, and begun her choice of the other—and time and the world had done the rest.

I wonder if she thought of that.

Twenty

Throughout my early years, from kindergarten all the way to college, there were angels scattered. The worlds they opened to me became the windows through which I saw my own.

Some came from the shadows, and could as easily have stayed there: wise, open-hearted men and women whose small kindnesses became like the dollars I hoarded in my pencil case—unearned, often unforeseen, a private cache. Others were more central, more constant figures, whose goodness I came to count on. But with all of them, one thing was the same. I was free to be a child.

Bea, who brought laughter into the silence. Mrs. Phillips, who offered her family as a refuge from my own and gave me a glimpse of myself. Jimmy, with his skating lessons and big-brother felicities. The last nanny, who let me know—by the end—that she understood.

And others, years later, when it mattered even more: my Uncle Jack and Aunt Peg, who steered my boat around every reef I aimed it at. My oldest brother, Archie, whose Kentucky home became mine for two of the most on-the-brink years of both our lives. A college dean, Max Cavnes, who risked his stature on his faith in me. And others, great and small.

But in those last, anarchic eighteen months of my parents' life together, my angels were mainly two: my mother's younger sister Ruth and her husband, Harlow Savage.

They lived in Riverside, Connecticut, less than an hour from the city by train. Their house, as I remember it, was large-roomed and sprawling, though it was probably neither.

They had land, though: a wide, shrub-bordered lawn, trees tall enough to climb in, a basketball hoop nailed over a leaning garage door. They had bicycles, footballs, ice skates, toboggans, a tree-house, a son, and a daughter.

Their son, Foster, was my age—roughly—their daughter my sister's. Excepting Massey Lake, it was my favorite place on earth.

It was in Riverside, with Uncle Harlow pushing, then running behind, that I learned to ride a bike. After that, anything—every-thing—was possible. There were no nannies, no boundaries, and almost, it seemed, no rules.

We spent whole days in Foster's "clubhouse," a disused tool-shed he shared with his best friend, Lance. We raked leaves and moved rocks with Uncle Harlow, shot baskets, raced bikes, played 45s—"Shrimp Boats," "Doggy in the Window," an unthinkable prospect at home—filled bags with sand to dam rainwater, ate dinner around a table (much like at Michael's) with everyone talking at once. Each day was different, an adventure. I went to bed tired.

There's no counting how many weekends I spent at Ruth and Harlow's. At least twenty, probably more, in the two years or so before my mother died. The closer things got to the end, it seems now in recalling it, the more often I went.

"We got you as often as we could," my Aunt Ruth says today. "Things were awful for you at home—for everyone. It was a horrible, horrible time. We couldn't stop it, we couldn't save Ellie. The best we could do was to get you kids out."

They tried to save Ellie. Their home was a refuge for my mother as often as it was for me, though seldom at the same time. She went there weekends from Silver Hill and from New York. They visited her doctors, rallied her siblings to her cause. One of them, my Aunt Patty, offered her home to the three of us if my mother would get a divorce.

They even found her a lawyer, a family friend, and booked the first appointment. But it was uphill every step of the way:

"We never saw her, those last couple of years, when we didn't talk about her leaving Archie," Harlow remembers. "We'd say, 'Ellie, you've got to get out, you've got to get away from the man, no one can live this way.'

"And she'd agree. She'd nod her head—'You're right, I know you're right'—but nothing would ever happen, she'd go back to him every time. It was like talking to a wall. She had places to turn. She just *couldn't* turn.

"It was too late by then, I guess. She'd stopped believing in herself. Maybe she'd stopped believing she was even worth saving."

But how did it happen? I ask them. Was it ever *not* too late?

"They lived in a dream world," Harlow answers. "Plenty of money, no responsibilities, and all that booze. It was a poison. It colored everything they did, everything they thought, the way they lived their lives.

"A beautiful woman, to Archie, was a social asset. Not a person—just an asset you wear for the world. He wouldn't even let her be a *mother,* for Christ's sake.

"He was a member of the *elite*"—and here Harlow's voice turns hard—"and in the families of the elite, mothers didn't mother, you had nannies to do those jobs. He wouldn't let her have anything to do with you, it wouldn't have fit the mold.

"He had such power over her. I don't know what his magic was, but he had *something*—she lost the will to say no.

"As time went by, she lost *herself*—her dreams, her sparkle, all the things she'd been. She was just so beaten down by the guy. All you heard was how stupid, how insignificant, how worthless she was.

"I remember once—she was at our house for the weekend—she came downstairs for dinner, looking as lovely as ever. And I told her so—'Ellie, you look radiant,' I said.

" 'Oh, no,' she said. 'No, I don't. You don't mean that, Harlow, you're just trying to make me feel good.'

"Even that—her sense of herself, of her beauty, her attraction to a man—even that was gone.

"It was awful. I can still see her that way. . . . We did everything we could except put her on a plane to Reno with Ruthie. And we even talked about *that*."

It is ten days before Christmas 1991. We are the last patrons in a brightly lit German restaurant in West Hartford, Connecticut, ten minutes from the home they have lived in since they moved from Riverside more than thirty years before. Ruth, a handsome, sharp-featured woman of seventy-one, has been silent for most of the last ten minutes, listening to her husband recall the details of her sister's debasement. Now she speaks, and the conversation shifts.

"You have to understand. Of the six of us, Ellie was the bright-est, the most spirited, the most beautiful. A magnificent lady, in every way. She could have had anything—anybody—she wanted. And she chose *him*. I don't know, I really don't. I never understood."

She is still shaking her head when Harlow speaks:

"She was just such an *exciting* woman. Dynamic, beautiful, with the sexiest voice you've ever heard. Both my brothers went out with her at one time, half my classmates [at Yale] were after her. She had it all, she had everything—brains, beauty, confidence, she could light up a room. . . .

"But she wasn't worth a damn by the time he got through with her."

No, she wasn't. She wasn't worth a damn. A firefly extinguished by a brute. No one who knew her, who even saw her during these times, could have failed to feel pity.

Now consider him. Consider my father: his days and nights those same six weeks—from late February to the first week of April 1952—that his wife was taking her last, assisted, stab at rescue, thirty miles north, her "tepid bath" in the mornings, her Ovaltine before bed.

He was sick. Physically and mentally, the body collapsing with the spirit. He was drinking now as never before. Day and night, alone and in company, his whiskey was his courage. He woke in the morning retching, with stomach cramps; in the pocket of every suit and bathrobe were packets of Tums. (I can't look at a Tums wrapper today without thinking of him.) His liver, which would land him in the hospital a year later—and would kill him in ten—was probably already shot. He had nosebleeds. He was underweight. His blood pressure, in the red zone for years, had never been higher.

"He is killing himself," my mother told her doctor.

Why? What had brought on this crash? And my mother's latest one, a month or two before? Something had broken them—had made them naked almost overnight. A stage set, collapsed like a rotted tree.

The Coes were planning to divorce. This was recent news; my mother told her doctor within days of her arrival at Silver Hill. I don't know when she'd found out—possibly that deerless November week at Massey Lake.

For most of an hour's session, she rambled on: Archie wasn't *really* in love with Vivian Coe, it was an infatuation whose time would pass; he wasn't her type, she wasn't his; even if the divorce went through, he wouldn't marry her. It wouldn't come to that.

Still, she wasn't going to put him "on the spot" about his plans. He might turn angry, even violent. It was best to wait it out.

"She is scared to death," her doctor wrote.

My father, I think, was on the spot already. His lover was leaving her husband; the ball had passed to his court. Were his passions as real as he'd posed them? Was his courage the equal of hers? A future awaited them. He had only to dispose of his wife.

He had probably said yes. A life with Vivian Coe was a fetching prospect. Well-born and moneyed, she believed in living well and had the means to achieve it. As a beauty, she was not the equal of my mother, but was striking nonetheless—and about the same age.

She was strong, at least outwardly. Severe and aloof in the poses she struck to the world. Alongside Ellie Douglas, she must have seemed a titan. She was a diligent mother; she would treat his children as her own.

But what an ordeal it would be. My father, with one failed marriage already behind him—the only divorce in three generations of Douglas men—knew well the tempest he faced. His first failure had been a wound on the family; there had been talk of "dishonor," a blemish on the name. But he had been a young man still, and not yet a public one. His parents had forgiven him. The moment had passed.

But now. To abandon a *second* wife, a fine, fragile woman of high spirits and good breeding (Granny was fond of my mother), to sunder a second home, leave two more children in his wake, as a man nearing fifty with a career in the public eye. And then to marry his mistress—the story was sure to get out—a Massey Lake neighbor and friend to his wife.

It would devastate his mother. It could cost him his career. There would be no forgiveness this time.

But none of this was the worst of it. *Ellie* was the worst of it. It would destroy her. She hadn't the courage to live alone. There would be scenes—ugly and public. He might have to take the children. There was a risk she'd take her life.

My father, for the first time in his forty-eight years, was face to face with the full weight of his choices—past and future. He must have felt guilty. He surely was afraid. He was a wreck those months.

He was in Albany weekdays through mid-March. Sometime that winter, no doubt to keep his hangovers at bay through the morning committee sessions, he began taking bennies. I don't know how much or for how long—"a lot," was all he would say.

Sometime before that, he'd stopped getting up in the mornings. The fall and early winter before he'd left for Albany, he'd made it to the office before lunch an average of twice a month. As often as not, he hadn't gone in at all. Clients sometimes called the house. They were told Mr. Douglas was away from the phone.

I remember that time, though not with any special feeling. I recall only that my father, who always before had gone to work in the mornings, suddenly did not; that he was there in the afternoons, in his bathrobe by the fireplace, when I came home from school or the park; that he was almost always unshaven, and that his smell was the smell of their bedroom in the mornings. I thought of it as the smell of sleep.

It occurs to me now that some of the worst of his daytime rages—the red star on my dancing school hat, a second, similar attack I suffered when I echoed Nanny's view that it was "bitter cold" outside ("Korea, the trenches in winter—*that's* bitter cold!")—probably happened during this time.

He was lower than he'd been in his life: sick, bitter, addled, depressed, and too drunk or drugged to go to work. Standing up to the Red scare in his living room, against a seven-year-old, at least proved that he still wouldn't run from a fight.

On a Sunday afternoon in early March, an hour or so before he was to catch his train for Albany, my father was home alone. A friend, Mr. Fletcher, dropped by without notice, just as Fritz Hubbard had done less than three months before. The two accounts are similar.

It was four in the afternoon. My father was "in his pajamas," Mr. Fletcher said. He was "mixed up." He knew he had a train to catch; he knew he had an appointment. He wasn't sure which was which, or how to find out. It wasn't clear if he knew what day it was.

Mr. Fletcher was troubled. He phoned Jack Pershing, who said that he too was "worried about Archie." He hadn't been coming into the office lately, he'd been missing appointments. Neither man knew what to do.

As before, nothing was done. Archie was "nervous," the two no doubt agreed. He had family problems, woman problems—a lot on his mind. He was hitting the bottle. They'd seen it before. Jack Pershing kept Archie's desk warm on Wall Street, and hoped for the best.

" 'He is confused, unhappy, unwell,' " my mother told her doctor in early March. " 'He is filled with hate. . . .'

"She tells of his shocking behavior toward their son Geoffrey, of the vile language he uses, of his literally telling the seven-year-old boy that he hates him. And equally wrongly, his absurd attachment and affection for their daughter Eleanor, age four.

"(As she describes Mr. Douglas, one cannot escape the pattern of a paranoid or pre-paranoid individual retreating into alcohol, getting more and more involved emotionally as his defenses crumble.)"

They tried to get to him. On a Saturday afternoon in mid-March, around the time Mr. Fletcher found him wandering around our apartment in his pajamas, my father drove out to Silver Hill for an appointment with the doctor—who devoted more than seventy lines of type to recording it.

It began badly: "He openly lied . . . said there was nobody else in either of their lives, woman or man, who was coming between them."

The doctor pressed on. My father rambled, then dissembled:

I went on to say that his actions indicated that he was unhappy. I wondered why. He then gave a long discourse on Roosevelt, the ideology of the Roosevelt regime, how he hated it. I told him I didn't think that was anything more than an elaborate rationalization, a manifestation of his own discontent. I wondered if he wasn't discontented for other reasons. Was he discontented with his wife? I asked him about sex. He said it was entirely satisfactory. It couldn't be that. I told him I didn't think we would get Mrs. Douglas well, and keep her well, until we got him straightened out, more contented with himself. I told him I would like for him to come to Silver Hill and stay. He flatly refused. Said that he could not accept the "stigma". . . .

I told him I didn't think that people who hated, who were as intolerant as he was, were that way because of things around them, but because basically they were angry with themselves. [I said] I had no idea why he was angry with himself. He said he didn't either.

And then it got personal—as it so often did where my father was concerned:

"I came out of it with the feeling that Mr. Douglas is a self-protective, self-indulgent, difficult, smooth, intelligent, shrewd, aggressive and ruthless man who hides behind a facade of assumed pleasantness, social grace and charm. And further, he is an egotist."

I don't blame the doctor—my father could do that to people. Still, there has to be some pity somewhere for a man so alienated he could send a psychiatrist to his thesaurus to vent his loathing.

Vivian Coe was in New York that winter as often as she was at home. My father was stretching his weekends at both ends.

"He lies, tells [his wife] he is taking a different train to Albany, then seeing the other woman . . . tells her to go ahead and have affairs, [that] he literally doesn't care whether she is dead or alive. . . ."

My mother, entrenched now at Silver Hill as she had never been before, went weeks without seeing him. But she knew his movements.

"On Friday night he was out with the woman, Saturday night in Boston with his oldest son, Sunday night back in New York with the woman again. She has the facts from the woman's husband. . . ."

Had she ever considered divorce? her doctor asked her. She'd mentioned the prospect, in passing, several weeks before. What were her thoughts on it now?

She froze and went silent. The doctor waited. For half a minute no one spoke. But when she answered, it was clear that her terrors were matched by her will.

She could understand, she said, how a woman could live with a cheater. Or a husband who beats her, or who drinks too much, or who lies every chance he gets. Some sins—even mortal ones—could be forgiven in the name of marriage. But a man who lies *and* cheats, beats his wife for asking questions, and hides behind the bottle through it all—"the combination, she says, is almost intolerable."

She was trying now. Her pride had deserted her, only her fear remained. Divorce, an unthinkable prospect only two months before, was no longer off limits. She opened the door wider on sex, on her husband's abuse—of her and me—the Coes, his disintegrating life, his power and its terrors.

Her doctors, for the first time in the year they had known her, saw room for hope. She had never spoken as she was speaking now. She was looking toward a future.

Her migraines had stopped. She was sleeping through the night, eating better than at any time since she'd been a patient. Her weight reached a hundred and fifteen, a two-year high. They reduced her sedatives, cut her morning dose of amphetamines by half.

She was gaining courage, or so it seemed. There was nothing left to lose, she told her doctor. She would make a stand.

Toward the end of March she came home for the weekend, her first in a month. My father was there: treacly and wet-eyed the evening she arrived, the way he got sometimes when there were amends to be made. It was a side I saw a hundred times; my mother, no doubt, a thousand or more.

The Legislature had just let out. He was leaving for South Carolina, he said, for a week of golf and sun. Would she come with him?

She refused. She would go nowhere with him, she said, the way things were. She wasn't sure she could even live with him. He had to change his ways.

He promised he would. She brought up Vivian Coe. He danced his best dance. He was in over his head, he said. There was "no future" in it; he was sure it wouldn't last.

I don't know what she said to that, but he left for his club in South Carolina three days later by himself.

At eleven-fifteen at night the Thursday after he arrived, my mother's doctor got a phone call at home. The caller was drunk, as usual.

"Talked with slurred speech, very slowly, was difficult to understand. The substance was that he missed Mrs. Douglas very much, wanted her to come down. Wouldn't I please tell her that he had called, that he wanted her to come?"

I picture him: alone with his bottle in his room overlooking the eighteenth green, drunk and desolate, railing at his impotence. Talking to himself, pacing probably, summoning his nerve.

Then calling: framing his syllables like a teenager home late on too many beers, imploring the mercies of a near-stranger he knows reviles him, waking him maybe—or his wife—at forty-five minutes to midnight on a Thursday night in March:

"He missed Mrs. Douglas very much. . . . Wouldn't I please tell her that he had called? . . ."

"It's late, Mr. Douglas. . . ."

Or: "Have you been drinking, Mr. Douglas? . . . I can promise nothing. I'll tell her in the morning that you phoned."

Or perhaps, worst of all: "You seem upset, Mr. Douglas. Is it *only* that you miss your wife?"

Never before, as wasted and desperate as things had become, had my father quite lost the handle on his power. It was his lifeline: the signature he wrote on everything public, his varnish against failure and the world.

He knew control, in all its colors. Charm and humor and persuasion. And when they failed—or were redundant, or doomed from the start—manipulation, cunning, intimidation, domination by force of will.

He wrapped himself in false modesty, grew dewy-eyed with hat-check girls—and when needed, no doubt, with a lover or a wife—shook hands almost longingly, lifted eye contact to the level of art. He orated brilliantly, laughed endearingly (when not cruelly), made a showcase of his passions: for life, principle, the rubrics of a better world.

Women swooned. Voters pulled his lever. I never saw a headwaiter who didn't bow and scrape. But few of them—only those, like my mother, foolish or unlucky enough to get too close—ever saw the truth. The emperor's new clothes.

His power was his contempt, nothing more. His contempt was his power. He loathed the world. Its covenant with him—St. Paul's, Yale, his mother's wealth and matronage, the "aristocracy" of his father's romantic longings—had long since been mangled beyond repair. He'd renounced it, by attrition. But the instincts it left still burned strong.

His piety was his machismo. No failure, no amount of wreckage, was enough to shake his faith in his place in the world. For every defeat, his anger turned more outward. His breeding—corrupted, mythologized—had become his touchstone against doubt. He was a zealot. In his sureness was his strength.

But not now. Now he was coming apart, or seeming to. His lover was leaving her husband, forcing him to choose between misery and holocaust. His wife, the last sure trophy he still possessed, had sent him south alone. She had allies now, too alien to counter, a new resolve he did not know. She was setting terms. The terms, until now, had always been his.

My mother stood her ground on South Carolina. My father—in a second phone call to her doctor, three days later—raised the stakes. He would take her to Bermuda, he said. She'd always loved Bermuda; it might do them both some good.

Her doctor advised against it—reminding my mother of the drinking that was sure to go on, the temptations she would face. She gave no answer. But it was clear that she was pulled.

Her new courage fought her old fears. Neither one prevailed— or rather both prevailed, each at different times. She told herself that she would leave him—then that she would stay, and make him change. Then that he *couldn't* change—that he was "killing him-self," as she put it so often—or that she was too weak, or too small a prize, to be worth his efforts.

"I hate myself," she told her doctor more than once.

And then, in the middle of it all, he would call or visit—or dangle Bermuda, the scene of her teenage springs—and a new life would seem to beckon. It was like what he'd done with the flowers—"We have decided that we are very much in love"—when she'd first felt her fear of him, thirteen or fourteen winters before. Or like her confusion with Bobby: "One day I decide I'm very much in love with you. . . ."

"Very much in love . . ." Bobby, Archie, and there would be one more. Whisper it in her ear, write it on a card, and the promises it conjured scrambled her will like the shock treatments had addled her mind. And just as impermanently. She was a slave to every tide that pulled her:

" 'I just get myself built up to the point that I think it would be better for me and the children to get out, and then he acts like he did Saturday,' she said to her doctor in mid-March. 'I just don't know what to do.' Tears come to her eyes. She wonders if she is getting anywhere here."

In the end, her doctor decided for her—the same day she told him she would be going to Bermuda.

"I am inclined to believe that . . . we have gone about as far as we can go for the present. I therefore told Mrs. Douglas she could leave this coming weekend, April 4th or 5th. . . . They will go to Bermuda the 19th."

There were reasons for hope. My mother's sister Patty had offered her home—in Princeton, New Jersey—to the three of us, if worst came to worst. Ruth and Harlow were standing by. My mother's resolve had never been firmer. She understood, or seemed to, the perils she faced.

She was discharged, the last of five times, April 4, 1952, the eve of their twelfth anniversary. As before, the prognosis was guarded. She promised to keep in touch.

She phoned a week later, three days after my father's return from Charleston. He was drinking, she said, but not to excess. His moods had been level; the time away seemed to have brought him around. They were leaving for Bermuda on the twenty-second.

Eight days after that, three days before their departure, the doctor phoned my father. He was just as sanguine. His wife, he reported, was showing a vigor he hadn't seen in years. They were getting along famously, looking forward to the sun and sand.

They were in Bermuda a week. On May 13, two weeks after their return, my father met with her doctor in New York. Silver Hill, for months, had been trying to ease him toward treatment. But he left few openings now.

"He has gained weight, face looks better, looks younger. Said he had no complaints with the world at all, said he was correcting his way of life. . . .

"He reports that Mrs. Douglas is very well. . . . Their life is going satisfactorily. I touched upon the other woman. He said it was a thing of the past. . . ."

He was lying. A phone call to my mother, a little patient prodding, would probably have exposed him. She lacked the art her husband had, to make a lie sound more like truth than the truth. She would have tried, no doubt: postured, concealed particulars, just as she always had. But she was a pushover for a sympathetic ear. Her doctor, I think, could have punctured the veil.

But he never tried. My father's earnestness was enough for him.

"All in all, Mr. Douglas was quite reasonable, looked better, talked better. I advised him to keep in touch with us, asked him to please have Mrs. Douglas call."

She didn't call. It would be a year before she called—and by then, the truth was too naked to be masked. A letter from her doctor, eight months later, went unanswered. He must have closed his file on her.

It's tempting, today, to think it would have mattered. That he could have helped her—even saved her—if he'd known the danger she was in. But I doubt it. It was too late. She was out of his orbit now, back into her husband's. Bermuda, whatever had happened there, had swung the balance Archie's way.

My father's powers were back. They would ebb briefly, one more time, but never fail entirely. Right or wrong, he always knew what he wanted. He was a hard man to keep down.

Twenty-one

I finished second grade.

I had no friends at Buckley to speak of, only boys who tormented me and boys who didn't. I was an awful braggart: made up farfetched stories, exaggerated small feats. If a teacher praised my reading, I would tell a classmate she had said I was the best in the class. When the school awarded me my AAU fitness certificate in the spring of that year—fifty-yard dash, standing broad jump, number of chin-ups—I spent half an afternoon at home erasing the typed numbers and replacing them with hand-printed ones, which, if true, would have made me a prodigy.

I destroyed the certificate in the process and exposed myself as a fraud. When I realized the finality of my act—the school wouldn't issue a replacement, I'd lost the only means to prove my prowess— I cried for half an afternoon.

I stole wallets, lied to teachers, bullied smaller boys. All this, coupled with the notoriety of my ear-stuffings, and the fact that I was—legitimately—the best reader and fastest runner in my class, made me a pariah. I hated Buckley, though I would be a sophomore in college before I understood that it wasn't Buckley I'd hated at all.

My sister. She was four that spring, almost a person now. For the first time, we played together.

One of my toys was a white canvas "house" with painted green doors and windows and a pointed red roof. It fit over the table in my bedroom so neatly that not a sliver of light came through at the bottom. Eleanor and I spent hours there, in a darkness of our own making that could be traded for light with the raising of a flap. Sometimes I brought my bed lamp inside, or my radio, and we pretended the things all children pretend.

Other times I bullied her. But rarely with blows. That would have been too easy to be fun. I was crueler than that.

"I never knew what to make of you," she says today. "Sometimes ally, other times tormentor. You were perverse—ingenious, though, in your perversions. You frightened me *so* much, you could seem so grotesque, so dangerous.

"You cackled like a monster, and made those horrible, demonic faces. I don't know *where* you got them. And you'd never stop till I cried—but then you always did. It was like you'd won or something.

"You were a twisted kid. I think I knew that, even then."

My power over Eleanor was a laboratory in which I tested, constantly (and consciously, to a point), the range and depth of my own aliveness. I never felt more vital, more sure or strong, than when I was torturing her. I was stronger and cleverer; I could reduce her to tears, then bring her back from them, as easily as a puppeteer moving a finger to raise or crumple a doll. She was my subject, the only permanent one I had.

I was insidious. Often after supper, I would prime her for bedtime by weaving long, labored tales—blended from elements of "The Telltale Heart" and Massey Lake ghost stories—about escaped madmen or murderous spirits from "beyond the grave," capping the effect each time with eye-rollings and evil moans. I would finish, always, with a promise of "death at midnight." Eleanor, in tears by now, would plead with me to "just be Geoffrey," but I would only leer and repeat my sentence of her doom.

Usually that would be all. Occasionally, though—just often enough so she could never know to expect it—I would creep into her bedroom after she was asleep, flatten myself by the side of her bed in the darkness, then reach up and stroke her face—light as a feather, from temple to chin—at the same time releasing the long, muffled ghost-moan I had perfected.

Eleanor would wake up screaming—but I would be gone, through the door between our rooms and back in bed, snoring lightly, before Nanny could get to her. I was never caught, and never admitted a thing.

From my tortures of her I learned both cruelty and compassion. In testing the limits of her terror, I teased myself with fear and guilt; in comforting her later—hair strokings, the offer of some small revenge ("You wanna hit me? Go ahead, hit me.")—I felt my power affirmed.

It was a cruel, sometimes dangerous game, but I needed it badly. I relied on it. It brought balance to my world.

For my sister there were no such scapegoats. She had only her dolls and toys to bully or to save. Alice, with red hair and dark eyes that opened and shut, to whom she told her secrets; a pink, frosted glass button-box in the shape of a chicken: "I used to sit in my room for hours and put things in and take them out, just to hear the sound the two halves made when they clinked together. I *loved* that sound. . . . I still have my chicken, you know. It's on Amos's [her six-year-old's] bureau right now. I don't know how it survived all the passages—I guess some things are just meant to stay with you."

We grew up in the same silence, shared the same meals and nannies and small symbols. But our visions of it are as different as the prisms we saw it through.

Eleanor, the porcelain doll on her father's ridiculous altar of sanctities—"Princess," "Nicely-Nicely"—wore ballet skirts and patent-leather shoes. She was made to wear nail polish, had her first permanent at four. Her hair was brushed and scented, she could curtsy before she could run.

I was "Goofry"—the bungler, the ear stuffer, the bully of smaller boys. I flexed my muscles in front of mirrors, practiced "good guts" when the iodine went on, shook hands with all my might.

Eleanor drew pictures—wonderfully well, on clean white sketch pads—of women in profile with perfect noses, later of princesses in peaked hats surrounded by castle turrets. My drawings were of battleships—crude, misshapen, and full of guns.

She remembers *Peter Pan* with Mary Martin, *The Nutcracker Suite,* a trip to the theater in Granny's Daimler with Owen at the wheel. My memories of the same things are overlaid with my terror of a mislaid fork at dinner, a "thank you" not spoken soon enough, an idiom—"bitter cold"—I hadn't earned the right to use.

Of her parents, from those years, my sister remembers next to nothing—her mother as "dark presence" who smelled good, her father as "lordly man" who bounced her on his knee. Neither one of them was much good at creating memories that would last.

She remembers an audition. She was four or five, she says.

"It was for the New York City Ballet, I think. *The Nutcracker* maybe. It was very serious, very somber, in this big studio with dance barres all over. There were probably thirty of us—prim little East Side girls in our tights and dancing shoes, being poked and prodded by these grim-faced people who never smiled.

"I remember them feeling my knees and calves, checking my spine—for straightness, I guess. They had their hands all over me; I felt like a poodle or something.

"I had to walk across the room and back with them watching me, I had to do pliés. . . .

"Then they walked away. Not a word, just walked away. I stood there for the longest time, waiting for them to come back. They never did. At some point I got the message—I'd been rejected."

Neither Eleanor nor I, in the end, would be our parents' child. But the molting happened slowly, a choice at a time. My sister, fourteen years after her ballet audition, would make her debut ("wryly," she has asked that I say) at the Autumn Ball in Tuxedo Park. I would buy my shirts at Brooks Brothers long after my St. Paul's days, and would test myself in bar fights until I was twenty-five.

In April of 1978, for my sister's thirtieth birthday, I took her to the Rainbow Room. We dressed in silk and tweed, ate veal piccata and drank Champagne, danced the two-step to "Everything's Comin' Up Roses"—in the spirit of a hundred Long Island deb parties—until close to midnight. We left giddy, but unresolved.

We traded the silk for jeans, took a cab to the grittiest East Village disco we could find, and bopped and sweated and drank bad brandy until nearly dawn.

It was a magical night—just the passage it was intended to be—with neither half shining brighter than the other. That was the beauty of it. We still talk about it sometimes.

My parents got back from Bermuda May first, a Thursday. At a political dinner the following night, my father announced his candidacy for a fifth term. It was a formality, of course, but his handlers must have breathed some relief. His slippage could not have gone unnoticed; he'd missed a third of the roll calls the session before.

But now—the Bermuda tan, the new vitality, the four or five pounds he'd put on: "It's the old Archie," they might have said. He would win six months later, as always, in a walk.

I finished school the third week of May. A week later we left for Massey Lake—together this year, as a family, only the second time in four years.

The trip was better than most. There was an argument in the front seat, about money, an hour or so out of the city. It might have come to something, but then my father got stopped for speeding somewhere past Albany, talked his way out of a ticket (one of three times I would see him do this), and was triumphant the rest of the way. We arrived, without incident, sometime after dark. It would be our last trip north together.

I don't know when the seeds of that summer were planted—if my mother had begun sleeping with Walt Coe before it started (in New York? in Bermuda?) or if, sometime that June under a moonlit sky with their spouses unaccounted for, one thing just led to the next.

He might have been her first adultery. More likely, her second or third. She was no innocent, though she would have liked to be. She probably *tried* to be ("your sometimes difficult-to-understand sense of pilgrim morality . . . the feelings inside you which you can try and fight . . .")—but she flirted like a barroom dancer, was married to a libertine, and would have wilted like a week-old rose deprived of her power to attract.

So my guess is, she'd had affairs. But always—always—*of the heart*. She was still too much the debutante-romantic to have given herself cheaply. Any man who had her—I'd bet a lot on it—knew something about rhyming quatrains and single red roses. For Ellie Reed, married or single, there had to be love in the bargain. Or at least the sound and smell of it.

However it happened that summer, once we got to Massey Lake the rhythms took over within days.

"They had the camp next door in the Adirondacks," her doctor would write the following spring. "Saw each other every night for three months—Archie with Vivvi, she with Walt. . . . Now it is a 'four-way deal.' "

"A sympathy thing," my father would call it—the cuckolded spouses seeking solace in each other's beds.

It's hard to argue with a verdict that plain: Sympathy to Ellie Reed, at that stage in her bedraggled life, was worth its weight in devotion.

It became, just as inevitably, more than that. Or so it seemed to both of them. By the end of that summer, as my mother would tell it later, she and Walt Coe were "very much in love." So too—if they hadn't been already—were my father and Walt's wife.

Not a whiff of this reached my senses. Not a false note sounded— I passed my summer as ignorant as a pig.

I was eight that July. Most of the reins were off me now. I could swim well enough to be trusted in the water, knew the woods too well to get lost. At least during daylight hours, I came and went more or less as I pleased.

It was a good summer, neither the best nor worst of my eighteen or so at Massey Lake. There were differences—I knew that much. They were *happy* differences, though, most of them, no less happy than the themes and habits they replaced.

I had a new friend. Billy Coe, the Coes' oldest child and only son, was four years older than I was—in sixth or seventh grade already—and light-years beyond me in everything. He could skipper a sneak box, swim the length of Massey Lake, lay a fly over the lid of a coffee tin thirty feet away. He owned a twenty-two (I think it was a twenty-two, I didn't know the difference), and knew how to load and clean it. He ran in a different crowd, and had since I'd known him. Until that summer, he'd barely nodded when I'd crossed his path.

But that year, for reasons I didn't know and didn't question— probably Billy didn't either—he became my mentor and sometime friend. It happened naturally enough, it seems in remembering. It never for a moment felt strange or strained. Only lucky.

We began, all of us, spending time at the Coes'. I don't remember how this happened, only that it did. If their camp had been across the lake from ours like the Hubbards' or the Stouts', if we'd had to row or drive to get there, it might have seemed less fluid, left a deeper furrow in my mind. But it was nothing, a five-minute walk at most: across our driveway, through the little stand of spruce and birch that divided their property from ours, then down the pathway that ran between the lake and the line of cottages that led to their camp. They must have made the trip as often as we did, coming the other way, but my memories of that summer take place mostly on their side.

From early June to mid-September, I spent probably half of my mornings, and at least some of my nights, at Billy Coe's. He had his own cottage on the grounds of their camp, which was larger than ours by far. In the little sitting room in front, where I slept when I stayed there, the walls were hung with the pelts of gray squirrels that Billy had shot and skinned and let dry. More than once, he took me with him into the woods above our camps, hunting for them. He taught me how to wait, not moving, behind a tree— sometimes so long my knees grew stiff from squatting—and how to aim and fire and reload. He taught me everything I would know about guns for ten years after.

I don't remember if I ever hit a squirrel, though I remember once thinking I had. But hitting or missing or just squatting all morning, I would have trusted Billy Coe to lead me through hell. As far as I was concerned, there was nothing he couldn't do.

Only once did I dare challenge him to anything: a fifty-yard sprint up his driveway to the main road. He beat me by close to half the distance. After that, I would have believed he could outrun a car. Outside of my father, he was the only real-life hero I had.

But it was more than just Billy. It was *all* of us—the easy rhythms of our days together, the certainty of our comings and goings as the summer wore on. I can still resurrect its snapshots.

Billy and I, crouching for squirrels in the woods, or raising the mast on their sneak box in the shallows off the boat house. Billy's little sister Anne, a big sister now, playing "horsie" on the grass with Eleanor on her back, or "tea" in the guest cottage with plastic cups and plates. Our two nannies—theirs was named Eva—with their iced tea and cookies in the little covered shelter by the Coes' tennis court.

And our parents—just back from the golf course or a bass-troll around the lake, mixing their old-fashioneds on the deck of the boat house overlooking the water, the flag flapping above them in the wind with a sound like stale bread cracking.

It was like that exactly, every piece. Of all my summers at Massey Lake, this one was the most nuclear, the most symmetrical. I missed, I suppose, the motley of other years, the pleasures of dashing from camp to camp never knowing whom or what I might find. I was bored, more than once, by the sameness of my days. But our summers—the summers of the kids—flowed as evenly and untouched by the grown-ups as four rivers from a common source: squirrel hunts, tennis games, "tea parties," the once-a-day cocktail-time rituals of dollar games and mothers' hugs. I played off Billy in their living room at night, let Anne teach me "horsie," took liberties with their parents I wouldn't have dared with my own. I felt a part of something better—safer—than before. I must have hoped, however dimly, that it would last.

I can only guess at the maneuverings. The four of them may have slept in one camp, with us—children, maids, and nannies—in the other, then switched a day or a week later. Or perhaps the lovers split up, one pairing to a camp, with the help and children divided between.

However they managed it—and whatever sordid, delicious gossip the nannies must have shared—there was never much need to be furtive. Sex at Massey Lake in the summers of the early fifties, among the nucleus of couples with whom my parents spent their evenings, was a currency of exchange. Sometimes consummated, sometimes leveraged, sometimes only implied, it was the *theme* of those evenings—as of a costume ball. It was their point. It was what you got drunk for.

An eight-year-old could feel it. The sexual energy at those parties—the lap-sittings, the plunging dress fronts—was as palpable to me as the smell of whiskey and cigarettes. I could not have called it by its name, but I felt its power: the naughty thrill of the bedroom jokes, the tightness in my gut when I nuzzled a neck that tasted of perfume. I never knew, I never even guessed, what happened after my bedtimes; but I must have known it was richer by far than anything that went before.

The Coes and Douglases were not alone. Half the lake was sleeping with itself those summers. Some of the pairings ended after a night, a week, or a summer; others broke marriages. Still others created new ones. One or two did both.

"It was a bad place," one survivor remembers. "A Peyton Place—there were lives destroyed."

All, or most, of this had ended by the time the Massey Lake community gave way to attrition in the early and mid-sixties. The misery, alcoholism, divorces, and suicides (there were three, including my mother's) decimated the circle of intimates and sobered those left behind.

But for those several postwar summers—the last good years for old money in America, the last years when my father's "good name" was still a tie that bound—Massey Lake was an enclave of corrupted privilege: backward, incestuous, a confederacy of tortured souls. There was scarcely a peaceful one among them, but the gaiety never ceased.

There is a picture from that summer—a gift to us from Nanny, when she left. Something to remember her by.

It is of the three of us: Nanny, my sister, and me, standing together in a clearing at the Coes' camp. The lake is in the background; a sailboat is moored just offshore. I am smiling slightly, darkly tanned, wearing an Indian-bead belt and blue shorts. Eleanor is holding Nanny's hand.

The picture was taken on Nanny's little Brownie, then pasted into the thin scrapbook of snapshots she left us with: "September 1952."

Nannies, sailboats, and sunny days. Untouched, summer-happy lives. Not a trace of madness in sight.

There were no secrets, that summer, among the four lovers. That much seems clear. They talked openly, as a group, about the knots to be unknotted, the loose ends to be tied. They resolved to leave nothing to chance.

By summer's end, they were close to agreement. By fall or early winter, as my mother would tell it later—flatly, as though reporting the pairings of a bridge game—all the pieces were in place.

"Archie has said he won't give me a divorce unless I tell him I am going to marry Walt. Walt's wife won't [divorce him] unless he says he is going to marry me. . . . She wants to be sure her children have a home. . . .

"[Walt] and [Archie] are good friends. . . . He doesn't object to [his wife's affair], doesn't want to have a divorce unless she is going to marry him."

"Archie has said . . . Walt's wife wants to be sure. . . . Walt doesn't object. . . ."

Did she *hear* herself? Four people, four lives—three votes and an absentee puppet. A figurine. She would sit where she was propped.

"Will you make a fourth?" they asked.

"They need a fourth," she said. "They can't play without a fourth."

It's hard to reconstruct such perverseness. And the record of that summer, told as history by my mother from a distance of nine months, is flimsy at best. Almost anything might have happened.

What *did* happen, what is recorded, is the madness of four people—aristocrats all—trying to believe that life could be molded on a plane somewhere beyond conscience and guilt, that responsibility could be nodded at, then dismissed, like a servant's wages.

Not the sex part of it. Not even the swapping. Adultery is classless, as popular among middle-folk as among the rich. It was more than that. It was the way they tried to *fix* it—to rarefy it, to assure clean hands and blameless hearts for all concerned.

Sometime that summer, amid all the openness and commonness of purpose, my father broke my mother's eardrum. She was treated in St. Regis Falls, then released.

Maybe Walt Coe decked his good friend Archie. Some men would have. But there is no mention of that. More likely, he didn't meddle. A wife was a wife, after all. A friend was a friend.

Things got no better. My father had tried, and failed, to trade his misery for a mistress. The abuse went on through the summer. By the end of it, as my mother would recall, "I had to learn to dodge."

She dodged when he swung at her, called the doctor when his fists hit home; found her way back to him when he left her in a pile by the road, took a lover—*his* lover's discard—when his appetites moved on.

She was nothing again. She had been nothing before. Before that a siren, with "the power to light up a room." Then nothing—then a fighter again. She would be a fighter one more time.

Pass," said the fourth, and closed the bidding.

"You're dummy, then," they said.

"I'm *always* dummy. Just once I want to play."

"You have to bid to play," they said.

She laid her cards on the table and walked from the room.

Twenty-two

The "four-way deal" limped on. Fall, winter, the spring of '53. It was more complicated now. Massey Lake had moved to Manhattan—there were schedules, responsibilities, appearances to uphold. My father ran for a fifth term that fall. Walt Coe's work kept him out of town. The lovers planned meetings as discretion and geography allowed.

The Coes' divorce was in the works. The Douglases—Ellie paralyzed, Archie dogged by doubts—had still not seen lawyers by May.

My father was almost never home that fall or winter. I asked Nanny once if he still lived with us. She said he was a "busy man."

"A businessman?" I asked.

She said he was that too, but that not all businessmen were as busy as my father.

"He makes laws for people and money for you," she said. I never forgot that. I felt as though she'd said he could run and fly all at once.

He got twenty-four thousand votes that November. His Democratic rival, a man named McCarthy, managed less than eighteen thousand. I passed out his handbills—"Honest, Sincere"—dressed head to foot in Buckley blue, to white voters in Central Park. One of them, a mother with a baby in a carriage, told me I was a "lucky little boy" to have such a father. I should be proud of him, she said. I said I was, and meant it. But I wondered where he'd gone.

The Coes never came around anymore, together or singly. I'd said good-bye to them in Massey Lake, the last day of our summer there, and hadn't seen them since. I must have wondered why.

Oddly, though, there were still some weekend parties. Not as often as before, no longer every week, but I passed hors d'oeuvres at least twice that fall and winter, and remember that my father seemed as much a guest as the Hubbards or the Stouts. He arrived each time when they did—I never knew from where—and left with them too, I suppose.

But for the hours he was there, it was as though he'd never been gone. He sat in his chair by the fireplace, told the same jokes and stories, and said good night to me with the same old feint-and-slap. Nothing seemed changed. But he was never there in the mornings.

He brought me a present one night when he came: a leather wallet with my initials in gold at the bottom and a five-dollar bill inside. It looked just like his and I loved it—but it was the surest sign yet that he'd come as a guest.

I can't explain those parties. They *looked* good, I guess, kept friends and appearances in place. The ship may be sinking, but the band plays on. My father saw things that way. My mother, I think, just went along.

Once that winter, on a school night when my mother was out, he arrived without warning around supper time. I hadn't seem him in weeks.

"A quarter says the butler did it," he said to me at the door, and winked, before he'd even said hello.

I was ecstatic—but had to wait, for what seemed like hours, while he made jokes with Bea in the kitchen and bounced my sister on his lap. He was in the best mood I'd seen him in since summer (the election may have just been won). It was his *safe* mood: the shallow, untroubled harbor between bathos and bile. It was a rare balance, and never lasted, but I could tell it at a glance. When he got like that, you could do no wrong with him.

We listened to "Mr. Keene," then to whatever came next. He paid me my allowance, plus arrears, plus the dollar or two I must surely have won. He was buoyant, clever, caring, warm. And utterly safe. I don't know if I ever saw him quite that way again.

He was gone in the morning. Or at least I didn't see him. I never knew if he had stayed the night.

My mother came and went. She was seeing Walt Coe now whenever he was in town, though he never brought him home when I was there—as far as I knew—and would tell me always that she was "dining with friends." I used to wonder how old you had to be before you stopped eating and began to "dine."

She was a zombie those months. She waited—a prisoner to her moods and pills, through empty days and nights—for Walt Coe's trips to town; shared his bed and comforts when he called, slept and drank alone when he did not, waiting all the while for a deliverance she could neither believe in nor imagine.

She drank in the mornings and at night, spent whole days in her nightgown, made long, teary phone calls to her lover upstate— then emerged, a phoenix in strapless dress and pearls, to hostess cocktails with a husband she no longer knew.

She'd lost touch with her doctor, got her pills now from her gynecologist uptown. They were delivered to our door weekly, by George in the mornings. Bea took them in to her, with coffee and the paper, when she rang around noon.

At least once that fall and winter, she was in her room for days with a headache. We doubled our silence. I saw her one morning in eyeshades through an open door. And still my father didn't come.

I arrived home one afternoon from the dentist with Nanny. My mother was in the living room—sobbing, on the couch. Nanny took me to her. I tried to resist, but couldn't.

She hugged me fiercely, as though she were dying—the way my father sometimes hugged—with a strength I hadn't known she had. She sobbed in my chest. The words came out like squeaks from a doll. Nanny, on her other side, stroked her hair and muttered in German.

She had broken something. A vase or goblet, an heirloom of some sort. She'd been trying all afternoon to glue it together. It wouldn't glue, she said—it was "ruined, ruined, ruined." She sobbed and sobbed. The mascara ran off her face in trickles and blackened my shirt.

Everything, everyone, seemed dying to me. Ghosts and figments, a half-alive mother. Longings for a gaiety I still believed had been real. I bragged and bullied and lied all day at school, came home at three and turned on my radio: "The Lone Ranger," "Gang Busters," Jack Benny, "Life Begins at Forty." It stayed on sometimes all night. I found a lump on my chest and worried that it was cancer; my leg cramps became polio; I took pills I didn't need.

Between January and March, as always, my father was in Albany: at the Ten Eyke Hotel, where he shared a room with Vivian Coe as often as she could make the trip.

But for the other six months between summers—the autumn before that winter, the spring that followed—I can't say where exactly he was spending his nights. All over, I think: the Yale Club, the St. Nicholas Club, the Hubbards', maybe once or twice a month at home. If the Coes still had their apartment by then, he must have spent some time there too, though their main home, and their children's, was a hundred miles north. But these are all guesses. He was a vagabond those months.

He almost never went to work anymore. Less than a day a month, my mother would say later, though she wasn't seeing enough of him to know if he was going at all.

He was drinking as never before. The bennies had started again. As little as he saw my mother that fall and winter, he slapped her around at least once. He hated her, she said. She hated herself.

Their friends were dropping away. Mr. Fletcher, since the incident with my father in his pajamas, had been too embarrassed to come around; he declined their invitations to the last two die-hard parties. My mother's ladies' lunches, a staple of her social life until the summer before, almost never happened now.

Even Fritz Hubbard. He told my mother that winter he didn't know how she took it. She should get out now, he said, before her husband's binges took a turn for the worse.

It wasn't the doings with the Coes that repelled them. There were few moralists among my parents' crowd. It was *everything*. Archie and Ellie had gone too far—crossed too many lines to be funny or fun anymore. They were a spectacle now, an embarrassment, together or apart. They were pathetic.

Spring arrived, the third season of withered hopes. Another summer loomed.

On May 17, two weeks before the Buckley "Prize Day" that would bring me home for three months and create a need for decisions, my mother called her doctor in New York. It had been a year.

How was she doing? he asked her over the phone. Never worse, she said. Is Archie drinking? he wanted to know.

"Everybody is," she said.

She saw him four days later. She was a mess—could barely complete a sentence without forgetting her thoughts. But she hadn't come only to be coddled. She wasn't alone this trip.

"Walt Coe is an attractive young man of thirty-nine, who fidgets, squirms . . . smokes one cigarette after another. I notice his forehead sweating as he talks. . . . He says he is very much in love with Mrs. Douglas. . . .

" 'I want to marry her, she wants to marry me, but we don't do anything about it. . . .' "

Ellie was terrified, Walt Coe explained. Paralyzed—"scared to move." The thought of divorce, the *process* of divorce, was too much for her. She was coming apart.

She would do nothing, she had told him, without the blessings of her doctor—which was why they had come. The session was to remain confidential. The bill should be sent to him.

She had hit bottom: couldn't leave, couldn't stay, couldn't make up her mind without the sanctions of a doctor she had barely talked to in a year.

"She was a vegetable by then," my Uncle Harlow remembers. " 'What'll I do?' 'How will I manage?' 'What will become of the kids?' It was too much for her. She had no strength anymore, nothing left of herself."

Her doctor's advice was frugal but sound. He couldn't decide for her, he said. But neither should Walt Coe. She was married—did she want to stay that way? That question should be her guide.

He added a coda. To go to Massey Lake in June with her husband, to reprise the madness of the summer before, would serve no end but destruction.

He said almost nothing to her lover. He was polite.

Somehow, incredibly, it was enough. I don't know where she got the strength to do what she did next, or why the well-meant homilies of a doctor she'd long since abandoned suddenly carried such weight with her. Possibly she knew, before she came that day, with what few sound instincts she still possessed, what was good for her—and only needed to hear it said.

Whatever her reasons, she was about to make her last—and best—stand. Of all the things I know of her, all the facts and memories and small truths that define her thirty-eight years, nothing else comes close to the courage, the pure resolve, she brought to that final battle.

It is a sad testament to a life: that its most deserving epitaph lay in its last, failed, attempt to survive. But it is the best measure of the poverty in which my mother left the world.

Within a week of that meeting with her doctor, she had canceled her plans for the summer. Eleanor's and mine, too. She booked me, on two weeks' notice, into a boys' camp in New Hampshire. It would be the only summer, of my first seventeen, that I wouldn't spend at least half of at Massey Lake.

For herself and my sister and Nanny, she rented a cottage in Southampton. They would move in the weekend of July fourth.

She phoned Ruth for the attorney's number. He saw her in New York the second week of June. They settled on "mental cruelty." He advised her—to avoid complications—to stay away from Walt Coe, or at least to keep their meetings discreet.

She almost managed it. They would see each other only three times between June and Labor Day.

There is no record of when or where she confronted my father. Only that she did. She had hired a lawyer, she told him; he should do the same. She let him know the grounds. One of them, she said, was going to have to move out.

I don't know what he said or did—if he threatened her, hit her, harangued about money, or tried to win her back. Perhaps he was relieved, or claimed to be, though if he was he wouldn't be for long. He moved out, officially, the first week of June.

Early the next week, he left alone for Massey Lake. For two months he summered as a bachelor, with the run of an empty camp: golfed, fished, partied, kept Vivian Coe's fires alive. I don't know what he told her of his plans—probably that they should take things a day at a time. That may have suited her; he was in no condition yet to make much of a husband. Still, she had to have known that the chase was winding down.

In August he left for Arizona for two weeks to see his cousin Lew, who had resigned his London ambassadorship three years before and was now a Tucson banker and confidante to the Eisenhower White House. Granny may have had something to do with that trip; she often relied on her nephew to talk sense to her son. The two men were close, though I suspect the admiration went largely one way.

I don't know what advice Lew offered his cousin, only that there were "family pressures brought to bear" to keep the marriage intact.

The pressures were not only on Archie. Sometime that spring or early summer, Granny had met with my mother for lunch. She wouldn't blame her, she said, for considering divorce—her son was sick and needed help. She would do her best to see that he got it. In the meantime, couldn't the marriage be kept afloat? For the sake of the children if nothing else?

My father drank heavily all summer. Sometime during his two weeks in Arizona, he woke up retching and bent with cramps. His cousin contacted a specialist in New York, who made the arrangements. My father flew east in late August, spent six days at Roosevelt Hospital under the care of a Dr. Field. The diagnosis was gastroenteritis.

He was advised to seek help for his drinking. The doctor suggested Silver Hill. He refused, was released on a Thursday, and was in Massey Lake the next night.

There is almost no record of my mother's summer in Southampton. I was there only once, for a long weekend in late August, the week after camp let out. I have a dim memory of small, irrelevant details: a modest living room scattered with wicker chairs, eating ice cream on a beach towel under a too-hot sun, a terror of jellyfish. My sister, oddly, remembers even less, though she was there every day for two months.

My mother spent at least a day a week in the city, where she met with her lawyer, trysted furtively—three times—with Walt Coe, and sought strength from the few friends she could still call her own.

Her will hardened now almost by the day. Sometime in early June, within two weeks of her meeting with her doctor and the new resolve that had come of it, she had written a letter to Jane, who was summering abroad with her second husband. The reply, long and rambling and full of love, was posted from New Zealand on June 28. It probably reached her the week she and Nanny and Eleanor arrived in Southampton. With its addition, the suitcase was complete:

> You, darling, are coming to the end of a long and terrible fight. It may seem at the moment like only the beginning. It isn't, believe me. You have at last faced facts. . . .
>
> If you'll only try now and take each day as it comes, without diving ahead into what horrors the next one might bring, you'll find you *can do it*! Don't for one moment let your thoughts be of tomorrow. . . . Reserve every possible bit of strength for each separate day. . . .
>
> Be a complete Scarlett O'Hara. Just say to yourself, "I'll think about that tomorrow," and somehow on the morrow it doesn't loom out at you quite so frighteningly. Oh Ellie, darling, how much I'd give to be with you now. . . .
>
> You know deep inside you there can be no peace or happiness this way. Regret for past mistakes is the most destructive

and dissatisfying emotion I know of—throw it out! You have learned by them, generally the hard way. Don't harbor regrets.

The reward that lies ahead of you is being able to give happiness. You have plenty of time for that, and those who know and love you know you can and *will*.

I'm awfully glad you saw Jack D. He's got a good head and fully realizes his brother's make-up. But for God's sake, don't let his mother give you a line about A. being a sick man physically and mentally, and how it wouldn't be cricket to divorce him. Balls and double balls . . .

El darling, if you think this is a lot of ranting on my part, I'm sorry. My only desire is to see you well and happy again. You will be, darling, but you must give yourself a break. Go stay with Mo-Mo, stay with Ruth, work with Sis, do anything, no matter how small or silly it may seem.

Sleep, sleep, sleep. I don't care how many pills you take right now. But take it easy on the liquor, it only magnifies the unimportant.

We will be back sooner than I thought. I don't dare name a date, but perhaps September?

Please keep writing me. There are many times I feel lonely and far away. Courage, darling, and take care.

Love,
Janie

I don't know if Jane made it back before the end. I've always assumed she didn't—that if she had, it might have turned the tide.

I hated Camp La Jeunesse—from the moment I got there to the moment I left. My cousin Foster was there with me (that had been the bait), but he made the cutoff for the "Chieftain" age group, I was only a "Warrior" and barely saw him all summer. Archery and mussel-diving were the two big sports, but my arrows never found the target, let alone the bull's-eye, and the mussels cut my hands.

My only distinction was the "Mexican Athlete" award, a wooden cup that went to the biggest bullshitter in the camp. I never knew if it was bestowed yearly or had been devised only for me, but I can still feel my shame when it was awarded, the last night of camp, with fifty or a hundred parents (including Foster's) howling in praise of Mr. Blagden's ragged wit. It was a miserable two months.

Sometime over the summer, my mother's lawyer requested her Silver Hill records. The hospital declined, but offered instead—on permission from her—to answer any questions he had.

My father must have been scared to death. It would all come out now. It could be the end for him—the "stigma" to end all stigmas, "Honest, Conscientious" blasphemed as the rubric of a fraud. For such a man, whose whole life had been a mask, there could be no crueler fate.

I don't know just what tortures he used to try to stop her, but for the last few weeks of that summer at least, from a distance and in person, he made her life hell.

His best hope, he knew—and his lawyers no doubt told him—was to defame her. To cast her as incompetent, cheapen her charges against him as the rantings of a woman on the edge. She'd always been fragile, an easy victim. To break her now, destroy her will to pursue the case against him, loosen the hinges of her reason in case she went ahead, must have seemed the only route. Nothing—short of her death—could have served him better.

One of them had to go down. There would be time later for kindness.

My mother saw her doctor Labor Day morning. She'd been back from Southampton a week. Eleanor and I were at Massey Lake, with

Nanny and my father, for ten days before the start of school. I remember nothing of those days, but considering the disaster that camp had been, they must have been the best of my summer.

Her will was failing. Her husband's torments were reaching her. If he even knew she was there that day, she told her doctor, he would use it to destroy her case. He was out to break her. But it was worse than that.

" 'He gets sadistic pleasure out of it,' " she said.

But she wasn't looking for excuses this time. She wasn't backing off. She'd cut her drinking to next to nothing, had lived her last three months with a single purpose in mind: No matter what the tortures, she was going to end her marriage. With or without Walt Coe, she would have a new life.

She had come this time for strength, not pity.

" 'I have to do it. . . . I want you to tell me I can. I can't take the abuse any longer.' "

She had set a mandate. The risks of failure were high. Her doctor read the danger. He put in a call to Ruth and Harlow—Ellie was at a crossroads, he said, they should stay in close touch—wrote out a prescription for Dexamyl (non-refillable this time), and made her promise to call within a week.

"I think there is a definite suicidal risk in this situation."

My mother phoned that Friday, September 11. She was feeling stronger now, she said. She had just seen her lawyer, things were back on track. She was on her way out to Ruth and Harlow's for the weekend.

The following Tuesday, the fifteenth, we got home from Massey Lake. My father drove us down, mostly in silence. It was dark nearly all the way, so we must have arrived late. He left as soon as we got there. I don't remember if he even came upstairs.

The next day or the day after—Wednesday or Thursday—my mother and I went on our last trip together to Best's. She bought me a blue blazer and a blue woolen bathrobe. I've forgotten what else. I probably got a haircut.

I asked her afterward, as I did each year, to take me to FAO Schwarz. She said no. We went to Schrafft's instead.

I ordered cherry pie. The waiter brought it with ice cream on top. I was befuddled. I asked him to bring me a separate dish for the ice cream.

My mother laughed and waved him off.

"That's à la mode, silly. You eat them together. That's how it's done."

"*What's* à la mode?"

She laughed again: "That's how it's done."

I didn't get it. "That's how *what's* done?"

It went on like this for a minute or more. She was delighted with her cleverness.

"It means '*that's how it's done.*' "

At length she took pity on me and explained. I was thrilled with my new phrase, used it half a dozen times in the taxi on the way home, then again on George as he was unloading our shopping bags.

"À la mode, George, à la mode. You got to carry them à la mode. That's how it's done."

"Don't pay any attention to him, George," my mother said. "He's just learned a new word—now he thinks he's French."

A day or two later, at three in the afternoon on Friday the eighteenth, Walt Coe phoned Silver Hill. He was in New Canaan with Ellie, five minutes away. She was in desperate straits, he said. She needed help now.

Her doctor was booked until five-fifteen, a little more than two hours away. He offered to see her then.

They couldn't wait, Walt said. They had to get back to New York. He didn't say why, or give a clue of what had come to pass. They would be in touch later, he said, and hung up.

The next call came from Ruth, nine days later: "Mrs. Douglas committed suicide, Saturday the 26th. They know very little about it, except that the maid had found her, she had taken sleeping pills . . ."

She was with Walt Coe the night before the morning she died. "She was worried about money," he would tell her sister later, and nothing more was ever asked. He dropped her home around midnight; the taxi waited, its meter running, while he walked her to the door.

Perhaps it was over between them. That would explain a lot— her tears in the elevator, why he took her home at all. He may have tried to end it the week before, then driven her out to Silver Hill when she seemed about to fall apart.

Just as likely, it was my father's terrors that drove her past caring that night. Or the shame she carried. Or the weight of all those unmet dreams.

She had wanted a life. She had reached for it—it must have seemed close. In the end, though, she chose between deaths.

Sunday morning the day after her body was found, a small gathering of the grief-struck—family and close friends—gathered somberly in the living room of our home. The Coes were there, and probably the Hubbards, and my mother's sister Patty from Princeton and her husband, George. Ruth and Granny and some others had come the day before. Bea served light refreshments. It was too early in the day for hors d'oeuvres.

My father was stoic, red-eyed, and shaky, but as sober as he'd been in months. He talked about details.

No, he said, there'd been no autopsy. Ellie would not have wanted it. He was sure, though—she hadn't meant to take her life.

She'd been nervous lately, there'd been problems between them, as everyone knew. She was under a lot of strain. And her heart had never been strong. It could have been a heart attack, he said, which is what the family would be told.

The Coes came and left as a couple. If you'd been there that day and hadn't known the story, you'd never have known they weren't: Vivian a rag doll, weeping on the shoulder of her husband as they stood under our awning, waiting for George to hail them a cab.

"Poor Ellie," she might have muttered, then sobbed, and held tighter to her husband's coat. "She was always so *alive*. Why did she do it, Walt? Did she give any sign Friday night?"

"Her life was the sign, Vivvi. She was the saddest woman I ever knew."

Twenty-three

It is a weekend night three years later. My father and Vivian Coe—now Vivian Douglas—are living with us at the River House on Fifty-second Street, five blocks south, in an apartment nearly the size of Granny's above a cobblestone courtyard with a fountain at its center, enclosed by a black iron fence. The doormen here are like soldiers; the lobby is all marble, leather, and glass.

Other things are different too. I am away now eight months a year—at a private boys' school in Massachusetts where I am taught discipline with multiplication tables and a barber's razor strop. Our summers now are divided between Massey Lake and Bermuda, where we live in a house with a butler and two servants on the seventeenth hole of the Mid-Ocean Club golf course. We come and go on cruise ships, where I am given dollars to play bingo and bet on races between wooden horses moved across the floor by men dressed in helmets and boots.

The string of nannies still come and go, but they are my sister's now. For me, in the summers, there is a Dartmouth boy named Pat

O'Brien who has been hired as my "companion" and mentor. He coaches me mornings on drives and putts and chip shots—my father's game—on the course outside our windows, followed by lunch and tennis lessons at the Coral Beach Club several miles away, where we are driven by the chauffeur who is also the butler, in a car that comes with the house. The Massey Lake camp we stay in for the second half of our summers is twice the size of our old one.

It is Eleanor's bedtime. Her stepmother has come to say good night.

A small black Bible, in soft leather with gold gilt pages, is propped in my sister's lap. It had been our mother's. A red satin bookmark divides it in two.

Our stepmother—"Mummy" by now to my sister—sits beside her on the bed. The Bible is open to the bookmarked page.

"Mummy, do you think this is where my mother stopped reading?"

The question is deflected. There are hugs and kisses, the bedside light is turned off.

Five minutes later, my sister half asleep, her father arrives by her bed. He has come for a reason. He is tender, but very firm.

"Princess, that question you asked Mummy—about your mother's Bible—it upset her very much. I know you didn't mean it, but please, in the future, try not to mention her name.

"She's gone, Princess. Let's try to forget her."

The Bible, after that, was given to me. I kept her picture in it, until I lost them both.